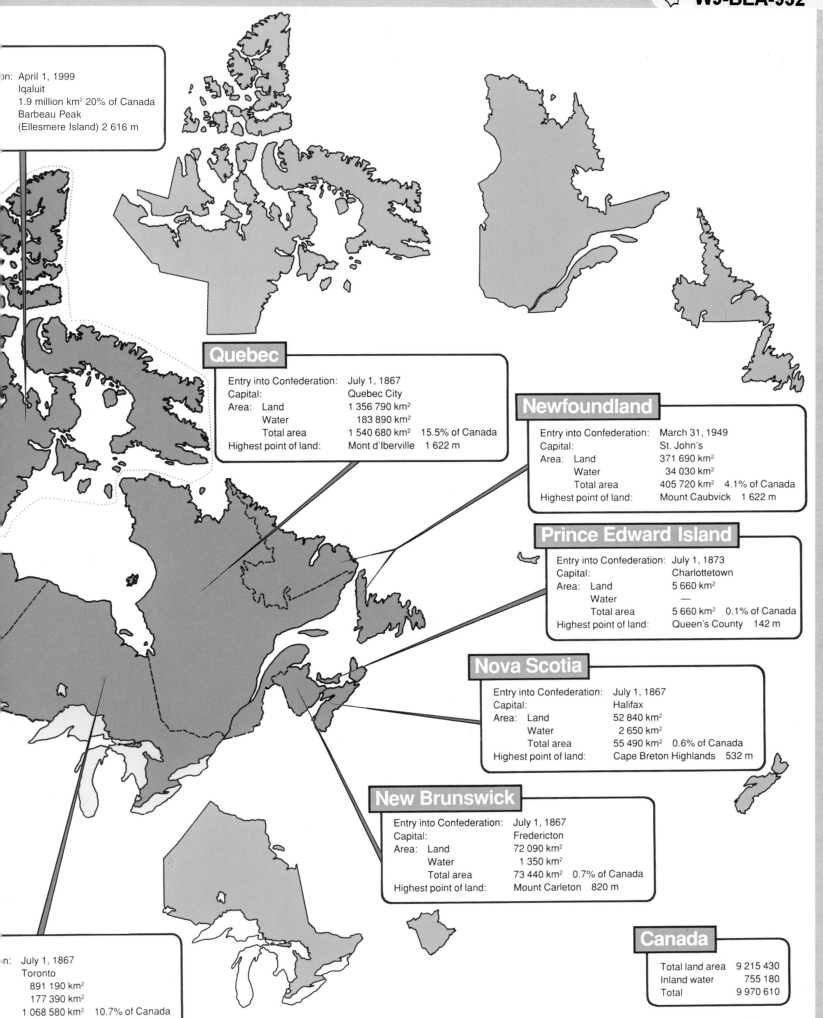

n: April 1, 1999
Iqaluit
1.9 million km² 20% of Canada
Barbeau Peak
(Ellesmere Island) 2 616 m

Quebec

Entry into Confederation:	July 1, 1867
Capital:	Quebec City
Area: Land	1 356 790 km²
Water	183 890 km²
Total area	1 540 680 km² 15.5% of Canada
Highest point of land:	Mont d'Iberville 1 622 m

Newfoundland

Entry into Confederation:	March 31, 1949
Capital:	St. John's
Area: Land	371 690 km²
Water	34 030 km²
Total area	405 720 km² 4.1% of Canada
Highest point of land:	Mount Caubvick 1 622 m

Prince Edward Island

Entry into Confederation:	July 1, 1873
Capital:	Charlottetown
Area: Land	5 660 km²
Water	—
Total area	5 660 km² 0.1% of Canada
Highest point of land:	Queen's County 142 m

Nova Scotia

Entry into Confederation:	July 1, 1867
Capital:	Halifax
Area: Land	52 840 km²
Water	2 650 km²
Total area	55 490 km² 0.6% of Canada
Highest point of land:	Cape Breton Highlands 532 m

New Brunswick

Entry into Confederation:	July 1, 1867
Capital:	Fredericton
Area: Land	72 090 km²
Water	1 350 km²
Total area	73 440 km² 0.7% of Canada
Highest point of land:	Mount Carleton 820 m

n: July 1, 1867
Toronto
891 190 km²
177 390 km²
1 068 580 km²   10.7% of Canada
Ishpatina Ridge   693 m

Canada

Total land area	9 215 430
Inland water	755 180
Total	9 970 610

SOURCES: The Canadian Encyclopedia Jr. *Hurtig*
The Canadian World Almanac 1999 *Global*

The Macmillan School Atlas

Third Edition

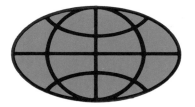

Ronald C. Daly

gage EDUCATIONAL PUBLISHING COMPANY
A DIVISION OF CANADA PUBLISHING CORPORATION
TORONTO ONTARIO CANADA

Canadian Cataloguing in Publication Data

Daly, Ronald C., 1932–
    The Macmillan school atlas

3rd ed.
Includes index.
ISBN 0-7715-8269-2

1. Atlases, Canadian.   I. Waller, John R.   II. Title.

G1021.D35.1991   912   C91-094642-6

Text Design and Illustrations: Full Spectrum Art

Maps : All maps by John Waller, except pages 96–97, 106–107, 121, 122–123 by Joe Stevens

Cover Photo: Masahiro Sano, Masterfile

Cover Design: Susan Weiss

Editorial Team: Anne Marie Moro, Carol Waldock, Carolyn Leaver, Tilly Crawley

ISBN 0-7715-**8269-2** (School)

ISBN 0-7715-**9092-X** (Trade)

    13 FP 03 02 01
Written, Printed and Bound in Canada

Acknowledgments

We acknowledge the financial support of the Government of Canada through the Book Publishing Industry Development Program for our publishing activities.

p. 1 The British Library; p. 2 NASA; p. 6, 26 National Air Photo Library/Energy, Mines and Resources Canada; p. 18 left, p. 18 middle, p. 24 top, p. 24 middle, p. 24 bottom left, p. 37 (Quebec), p. 39 top left, p. 39 top right, p. 43 top right Robert Waldock; p. 18 (illustration) Anne Stanley; p. 18 right, p. 19 middle Jennifer Walti-Walters; p. 19 left, p. 37 (Regina) S.P.M.C.— Photographic Services Agency; p. 19 right, p. 43 bottom left Province of British Columbia; p. 20 top Tokyo Stock Exchange, Tokyo, Japan; p. 21 top Dilip Mehta © ACDI/CIDA; p. 20 bottom Ellen Tolmie © ACDI/CIDA; p. 21 bottom, p. 96 (3), p. 97 (5), p. 99 top left, p. 101 (3), p. 107 bottom Victor Englebert; p. 22 Embratur, Brazil; p. 23 top Patricio Baeza; p. 23 bottom, p. 99 bottom left, p. 99 bottom right, p. 107 middle Robin White/Fotolex; p. 24 bottom right U.S. Information Service; p. 25 top, 25 bottom right Richard Hartmier/Fotolex; p. 25 middle E.B. Waldock; p. 25 bottom left, p. 90 Courtesy of Costa Rica National Tourist Bureau; p. 27 Produced from USAF DMSP (Defense Meteorological Satellite Program) film transparencies archived for NOAA/NESDIS at the University of Colorado, CIRES/Campus Box 449, Boulder, CO 80309; p. 29 top, p. 31 middle left, p. 123 Industry, Science and Technology Canada; p. 29 middle Lee Battalia/United States Information Service; p. 29 bottom Courtesy of Alfonso Nieto, Pres Attache, Consulado General de Mexico; p. 31 top left Dynese Griffiths/Network Stock Photo File; p. 31 top right Ministry of Natural Resources; p. 31 middle right Florida Department of Commerce, Division of Tourism; p. 31 bottom Bill Ivy; p. 37 Courtesy of the Department of Development, Government of Newfoundland and Labrador/Wayne Sturge; p. 37 Nova Scotia Tourism & Culture; p. 37 Prince Edward Island Tourism Photo/ Wayne Barrett; p. 37 Keith Minchin/Visitors and Convention Bureau/Frederiction; p. 37 Metropolitan Toronto Convention & Visitors Association; p. 37 Photo/Fred Bruemmer, Valan Photos (Iqaluit); p. 37 Alan Zenuk/Industry, Science and Technology Canada (Winnipeg); p. 37 Photo courtesy of the City of Edmonton; p. 37, p. 107 top M. Herweier (Victoria); p. 37 Bruce Sekulich/Government N.W.T.; p. 37, 85 left W. Towriss (Whitehorse); p. 39 bottom Ministry of Forests, Province of British Columbia; p. 42 top left Maynard Switzer; p. 42 bottom right Canapress Photo Service/Ryan Remiorz; p. 42 middle right Bob Anderson; p. 42 top right Mir Lada; p. 43 middle left The Toronto Star/P. Gower; p. 43 top left Canada Wide Feature Services/The Toronto Sun/Bill Sandford; p. 55 Department of Fisheries and Oceans, Pacific Region; p. 85 right Katsunori Nagase/Government N.W.T.; p. 85 bottom Photo/Fred Bruemmer, Valan Photos; p. 87 top left Photo courtesy of the Port Authority of New York and New Jersey; p. 87 top right Greater Houston Chamber of Commerce; p. 87 bottom San Francisco Convention and Visitors Bureau; p. 89 Mexican National Tourist Council; p. 91 © A. & J. Verkaik/Skyart; p. 92 G.L. Palacky; p. 99 top right, 101 bottom South African Tourism Board; p. 102 Canapress Photo; p. 106 left ACDI/CIDA; p. 106 right David Barbour © ACDI/CIDA; p. 108, 109 (2) Courtesy of the Australian Tourist Commission; p. 111 (2) Ian W. D. Dalziel; p. 113 top left, p. 122 (3), p. 123 top Indian and Northern Affairs Canada; ßp. 113 top right George Calef/Government N.W.T.; p. 113 bottom Lothar Dahlke/Government N.W.T.; p. 121 left "West Coast Indians Returning from the Hunt" by Thomas Mower Martin/Collection of Glenbow Museum, Calgary, Alberta 56.27.8; p. 121 right National Archives of Canada C-33615/"A Buffalo Pound" drawn by Lieut. Back, Engraved by Edw. Finden.

Contents

*Change is a major global expectation today. Atlas publishers are hard pressed to include the most recent boundary and name changes. All changes known at the time of printing have been included.

Introduction to Maps

Have you ever wondered where maps came from?

Long ago, soldiers, seamen, merchants, and other travellers created maps as a way of recording the places they had visited and the routes there and back. It is amazing how accurate some of those early maps were considering the tools used at the time by these mapmakers. Maps took shape slowly as people used them to find their way around. They became more and more accurate as mapmaking tools improved.

Believe it or not, some of the earliest maps were recorded on bark or animal skins. Others were burned or cut into bone or wood. Later maps were recorded on parchment, papyrus, or paper.

When collections of maps were joined together in one book, such as *The Macmillan School Atlas*, the book became known as an atlas. The idea of binding together a variety of up-to-date maps into a book began in Rome in the sixteenth century—over 400 years ago. It was the idea of a man named Antonio LaFriei, who saw an opportunity to create special map collections for his customers.

Atlases were named after the god Atlas of Greek mythology. Read a few Greek myths to find out why Atlas was doomed forever to carry the world on his shoulders.

Using an atlas is one way to find interesting and important information about places and people.

The Earth

When astronauts first landed on the moon, they looked back to Earth and saw a round, ball-like shape. From the moon, Earth looked like a giant globe of many colours. This proved again that the planet where you live is not flat, as was once thought, but is a **sphere**. Maps, however, are flat. Flat maps tell us many things about places on Earth. But only a globe correctly shows the size, shape, and position of land and water areas as they really are.

Many special locations are marked on a globe. Examine a globe carefully to discover the North and South Poles. Have you found them? Halfway between the poles is an imaginary line called the equator. The distance around the Earth at the equator is approximately 40 100 km. This distance is as far as travelling across Canada—seven times!

The Earth's **diameter** at the equator is roughly 12 760 km, while the diameter north to south is 12 710 km. As you can see by these measurements, the Earth is not perfectly round but is slightly flattened at the poles. However, because this flattening is so small compared with the Earth's total size, most people think of Earth as being ball-like in shape.

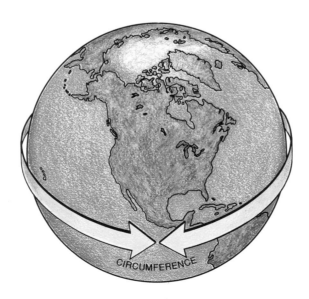

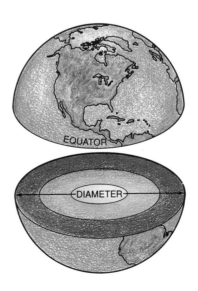

Hemispheres

How much of the globe can you see when you hold it in your hands? Only half of it shows at any one time. The half that you see is called a **hemisphere**, which means "half a sphere." No matter how you hold the globe, there will always be two hemispheres, the half that you see and the other half that you do not see.

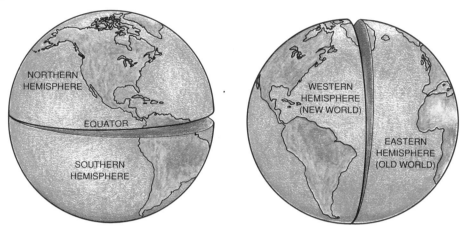

There can be many hemispheres. By moving the globe in your hands, you can see different halves. Remember there is always an opposite side to the one that you are looking at. When placed together, two hemispheres will always make a complete sphere.

If you could cut along the equator, the globe would separate into **northern** and **southern hemispheres**. If you could cut through the Atlantic and Pacific Oceans, then the globe would separate into the Eastern and Western Hemispheres.

Other important hemispheres are the **land hemisphere** and the **water hemisphere**. The land hemisphere is centred on a line drawn from Brussels to Paris. It contains almost 85 percent of all land on the Earth's surface. The centre of the water hemisphere is located near New Zealand.

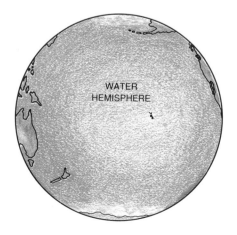

Latitude

Distances north and south of the equator are measured in degrees of latitude. Examine a globe and locate the equator again. The equator is the imaginary line that cuts the globe in half between the North and South Pole. Above and below the equator are other lines drawn in the same manner. Can you find them? These lines are parallel to the equator and are called **parallels of latitude**.

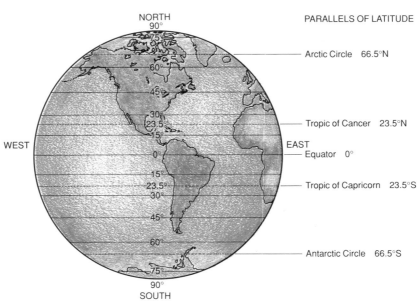

Each of the parallel lines of latitude are numbered in degrees. As you look at the lines above and below the equator, can you see that each parallel's number is followed by an N or S? This indicates whether you are looking at the Northern or Southern Hemisphere. The number of each parallel increases from 0° (the equator) to 90° as you move toward the North or South Pole. The latitude of the North Pole is 90°N. At the South Pole it is 90°S. No place on the globe can be more than 90° north or south. Why is this?

All locations along each parallel are the same distance from the equator. If the latitude of a place is 45°N, you know that place is on a line halfway between the equator and the North Pole. A place which has a latitude of 45°S is midway between the equator and the South Pole.

One degree of latitude is approximately 113 km. Once you know the latitude of any given position, you will be able to calculate its distance from the equator. Since all places along the same latitude are directly east or west of each other, parallels of latitude may be used to set east-west direction.

Some parallels have special names. Can you find the Arctic Circle and the Tropic of Cancer that lie north of the equator? The Antarctic Circle and the Tropic of Capricorn are south of it.

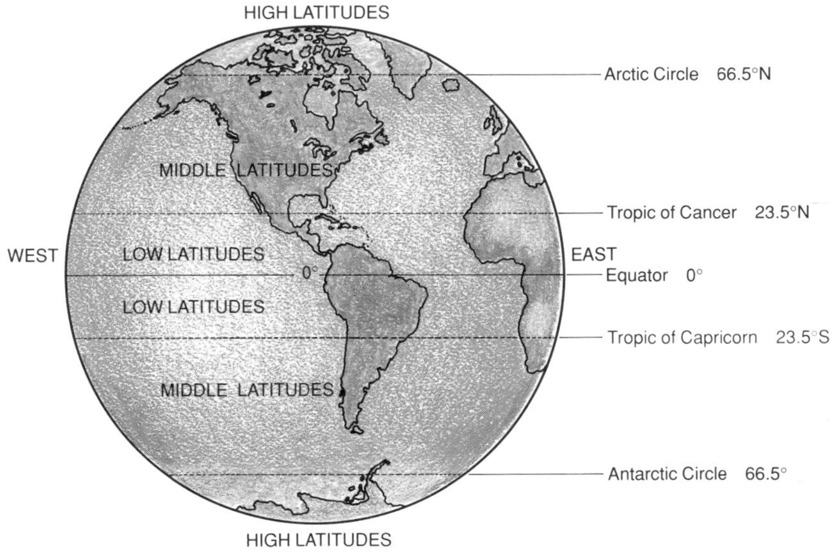

The parallels also divide the Earth into **low**, **middle**, and **high latitudes**.

Longitude

To help locate places on the Earth's surface, a second set of lines is drawn on a map or globe. These lines reach from the North to the South Pole.

They are called **meridians of longitude**. Unlike parallels of latitude, meridians are not parallel to one another but join at the poles. Can you see how each meridian is the same length as every other meridian?

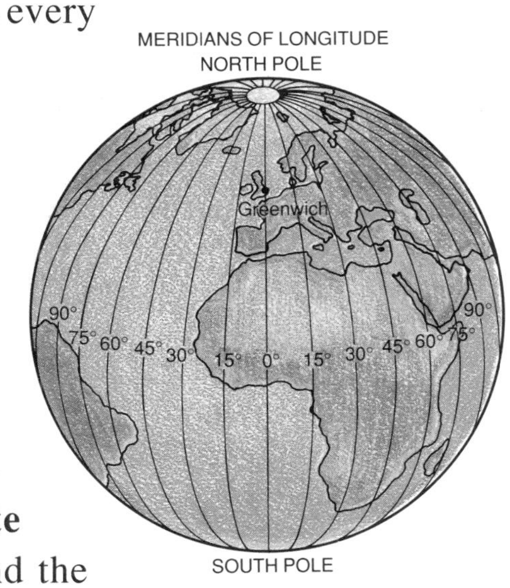

Because there is no real difference between meridians, mapmakers had to agree upon which one to number 0. If you trace your finger along the line numbered 0, you will see that it passes through Greenwich, England. It is called the **prime meridian**. The meridian on the opposite side of the globe is called the **International Date Line**. Together, the prime meridian and the International Date Line divide the Earth into eastern and western hemispheres.

As you turn the globe in your hands you can see that the meridians of longitude are also numbered in degrees. Meridians measure distances in degrees east or west of the prime meridian. Going east of the prime meridian, the lines are numbered to 180°E. Going west they are numbered to 180°W.

The parallels of latitude and the meridians of longitude on maps together create a network of lines called a **grid**. A grid is used to locate particular places. When you know both the latitude and longitude of a given place, you are able to locate its exact position.

Even when a place is not located precisely where lines cross, you can still discover its approximate position. When using the grid for finding any given place, remember latitude is always stated before longitude. **Latitude and longitude give location.**

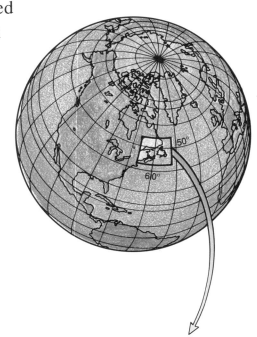

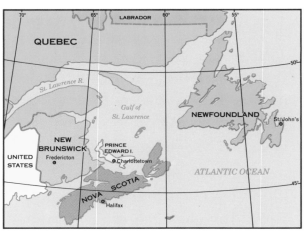

Gazetteer

At the back of the atlas is a section containing a list of all the names of places shown on the maps in this book. This section is called the **gazetteer** or **index**. A gazetteer includes all the information you need for locating places. Places are listed alphabetically. What other information are you given?

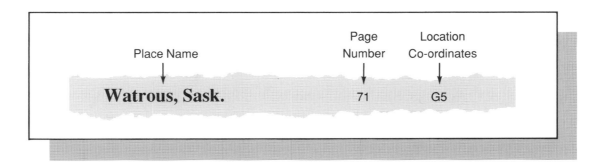

Place Name   Page Number   Location Co-ordinates

Watrous, Sask.   71   G5

Look in the gazetteer for the name of the place where you live. Use this information to locate your hometown on a map in the atlas. Try this activity again looking up places that you know about or that you have visited.

Great Circles

Every circle drawn around the globe divides it into two hemispheres. These circles are called Great Circles. The segment of a Great Circle that passes through any two places is the shortest distance between those places. Transportation pathways based on Great Circles are called **Great Circle Routes**.

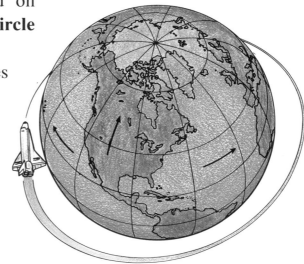

Ships often follow circle courses to reach their destination by the shortest possible route. Airplanes may follow circle routes over land unless they are forbidden to do so by certain countries.

Time

Every twenty-four hours the Earth makes one complete turn from west to east. It turns around an imaginary line that passes through the centre of the Earth from the North Pole to the South Pole. This line is known as the Earth's **axis**.

We depend on the Sun for our heat and our light. As the Earth spins on its axis, the part that faces the Sun receives heat and light. It is day on this part of the Earth. The part that is turned away from the Sun is cool and is in darkness. It is night on this part of the Earth.

Does the Sun really "rise in the east and set in the west"? No. The Sun never moves. Because the Earth turns on its axis from west to east, it may look as if the Sun were rising in the east. Our last view of the Sun is in the west, as the Earth turns away from it.

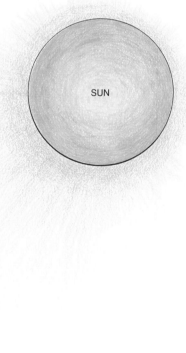

SUN

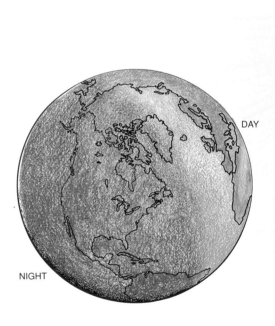

DAY

NIGHT

All places on Earth do not have noon at the same time, because of the way the Earth spins on its axis. Every twenty-four hours it turns 360° —15° each hour. Noon where you live would be one hour later than in a place fifteen degrees east of you.

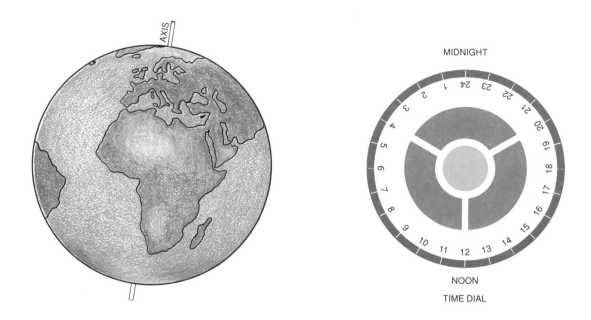

To avoid the confusion there would be if every place used its own time, **time zones** have been established. All places within a time zone have the same time. There are twenty-four of these time zones — one for every fifteen degrees.

The borders of time zones do not always follow meridians, but often follow the borders of countries or of provinces and states.

Canada's time zones are shown on the map below.

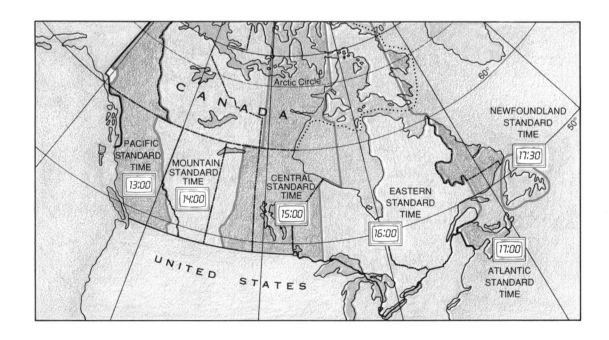

The Change of Seasons

As the Earth revolves in an orbit about the Sun, its axis is tilted at an angle of 23.5°. This causes changes in the length of time places receive heat and sunlight. That is why seasons change each year. In summer, the Northern Hemisphere tilts toward the Sun to receive its direct rays. As a result the days are longer and have greater heat. In winter, the Northern Hemisphere tilts away from the Sun. Then the days are shorter and have less heat. In spring and fall the Earth's axis points neither toward nor away from the Sun.

In the Southern Hemisphere the seasons are opposite to our own. Look at a globe and see if you can explain why this happens.

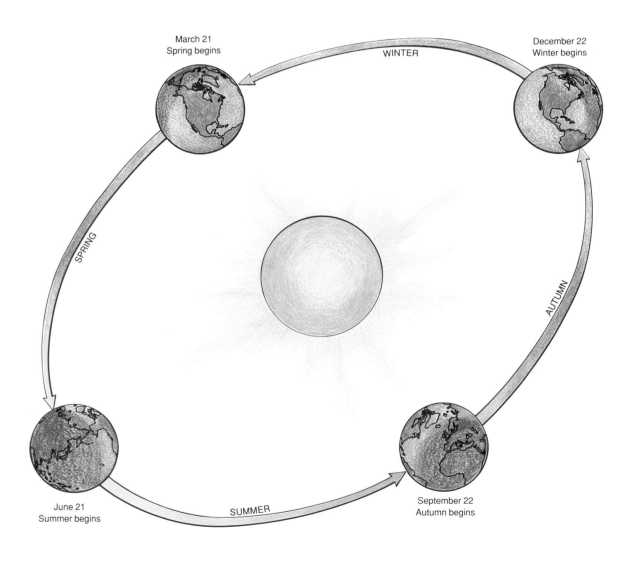

The Earth and the Moon

The Moon is the brightest object in our night sky. When you look at it from Earth it seems to be as large as the Sun. But it is not as large as the Sun. It looks larger only because it is closer to Earth. The Moon's distance from Earth is about 384 400 km. This is about ten times the distance around the Earth at its equator.

If you were watching the Moon through a telescope, you would see that it travels from west to east. As it travels, the Moon appears to change its shape. These changes are called **phases** of the Moon.

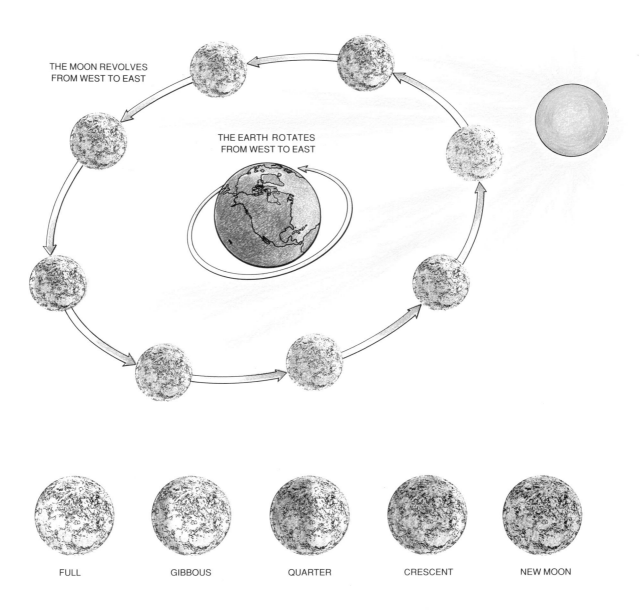

THE MOON REVOLVES FROM WEST TO EAST

THE EARTH ROTATES FROM WEST TO EAST

FULL   GIBBOUS   QUARTER   CRESCENT   NEW MOON

Mapping

A **map** is a drawing of all or a part of the Earth's surface seen as if you were looking down on it from above. Maps attempt to present Earth's natural or built features on a flat surface. We know a globe gives us the truest picture of any land or water area, but we also know it is not as convenient to use as a map is. Imagine taking a globe along with you every time you and your family went on a special trip!

Mapmakers have tried many different ways of drawing the rounded surface of Earth on a flat piece of paper. But they have discovered that no matter what way they tried, they could not flatten a curved surface without causing changes to the shape of the continents.

The globe is the only way of showing how the Earth looks to true scale. The diagram below shows one way to make a map. If a globe were cut open along its lines of latitude and longitude and then pressed flat, it would be a map.

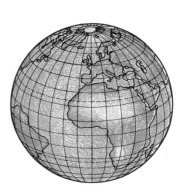 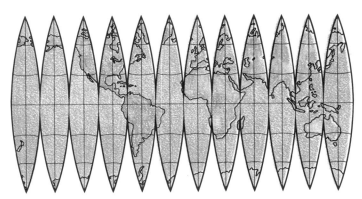

Map Projections

Each different way of transferring details from a globe to a sheet of paper is called a **map projection.** There are many kinds of map projections; each one is designed for a special reason. The illustrations on page 13 show three different styles of map projections: the Robinson projection, the Mercator projection, and the Peters projection.

Mapmakers often use mathematics to work out a projection. Can you see how in each illustration the shapes of the continents differ from the way they appear on the globe? These changes are called **distortions.** There is no way to make a flat map without some distortion.

Robinson projection

National Geographic uses this projection that has a distortion of less than 20 percent for most of the world continents.

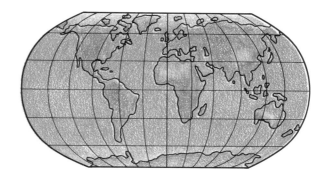

Mercator projection

Navigators and pilots prefer to use this projection because the great circle routes are shown as straight lines rather than as curved lines. However, note how northern and southern latitudes appear very much bigger than they really are.

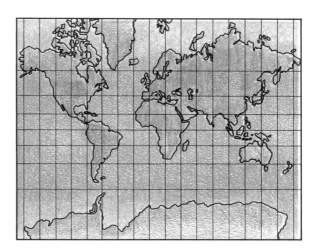

Peters projection

The United Nations prefers this projection because it shows developing countries clearly. All countries are shown with accurate areas but, as you can see, some shapes are distorted.

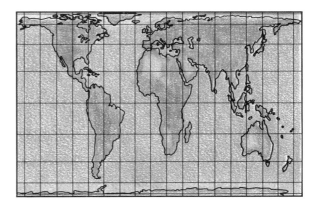

When you examine maps in this atlas, you will see differences from one map to another. For example, even using the same projection, maps of a large area (such as that found on page 28) will show more distortion than maps of a smaller area (page 71). Why do you suppose that happens?

No single projection can be drawn to show accurately all four qualities—area, shape, distance, and direction—at the same time. Only a globe can do that.

Understanding Maps

There are different kinds of maps. Some maps are designed to show you where certain places are in the world. These are called **general maps**. Other maps show specific information about things such as transportation routes or what vegetation is like in a certain area. These are called **thematic maps**. Information on a thematic map is usually coded with colour and shapes.

An example of a general map can be found on page 36. An example of a thematic map can be found on page 38. Can you find other examples?

Scale

It would be impossible to draw a map the same size as the area it shows. Imagine how much paper you would need to map your city or town! For this reason, all maps are drawn to **scale**. An exact distance on the map stands for a certain (much larger) distance on the ground. Every map has some statement of scale to help you estimate distances.

Maps are drawn to different scales. One map may show an area twice as large as the area shown on another map. A one-page map of a large area of land and water, such as Canada, must be drawn to a small scale, so that the large area will fit on the page. A one-page map of a much smaller area, such as Manitoba, can be drawn at a larger scale. A large-scale map shows more detail. Look at Manitoba on atlas page 36 and on page 69. What difference do you see? What is the scale of each of these maps?

Scale is shown in various ways. A linear scale uses a rule or line divided into equal segments. Each segment represents a specific distance on the ground. A second method states the scale as the ratio between the actual distance and the distance on the map. If a mapped area was drawn at one

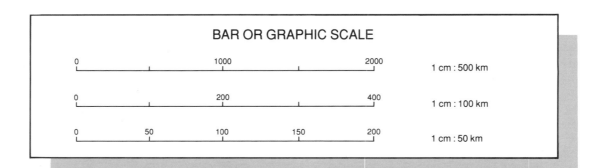

quarter the actual size, the ratio would be expressed at 1:4. If an area was mapped at one thousandth of its actual size, the ratio would be 1:1000. A third method of expressing scale is simply in a statement: "One centimetre represents ten kilometres.

Unless you look closely, the linear scales on maps may all look the same. The line used for the scales on the maps may all be the same length. But this length may represent entirely different distances from map to map. On one map 1 cm might represent 100 km. On a second map a line of exactly the same length might represent only 50 km. See how many different linear scales you can find in this atlas.

Legend

Different maps give different kinds of information. To find out what a map is all about, look at its title. The title will tell you the name of the area or region shown on the map, and what kind of map it is that you are looking at. The **legend** will explain the symbols used on the map.

Each **colour** used on a map usually has its own special meaning. But every map has its own special colouring. A colour used on one map may mean something completely different when used on another map.

A legend shows the **symbols** used on the map. They may represent natural features such as a river or a lake, or features made by humans such as a road or a pulp and paper mill.

Map symbols change meaning from one map to another, just the way colours do. It is very important to use the legend if you want to uncover the information on each map.

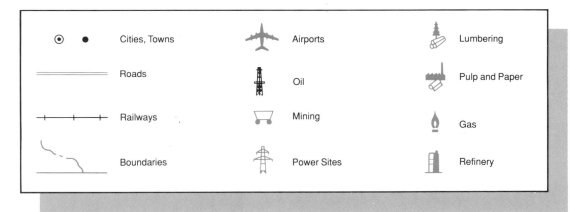

Example of a Legend

Elevation

When mapmakers want to show different heights of land on their maps, they use **contour lines**. Contour lines join together places of the same height. The spaces between the contour lines show heights which are at the same level. Where the contour lines are very close together the slope of the land is steeper than in areas where the contour lines are widely spaced.

Look at these pictures carefully. Can you see that the heights of land are not the same everywhere? Some lands are slightly above sea level. These are called **lowlands**. Other lands are higher and are called **middlelands**. The highest lands are called **highlands**.

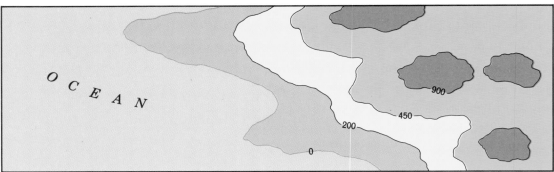

Above you see a map of the same area. Can you find all the places where the land 200 m above sea level is joined by the same line? Follow this line with your finger to make a complete circle.

Colour

Colour is often used to show heights of land. All the land from sea level at 0 m to 200 m above sea level is shown in this atlas as green. The land 200 m to 450 m is coloured yellow. The land 450 m to 900 m is brown. What colour is used when showing heights of land above 900 m?

Direction

Because a large map is usually hung on a wall, you may make the mistake of thinking direction north is always at the top of the map. But "up" and north on a map may not necessarily be the same thing.

This is why most maps have a special symbol to show **direction**. In this atlas the direction north is shown like this.

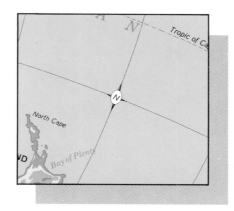

Once you know where north is, you should know where all the other directions are for that particular map. Can you find them? When you face north, south is in the opposite direction, east is to the right. Where is west?

You can use the grid lines of a map to find the four main directions too. Parallels of latitude always lie in an east-west direction. All meridians of longitude run in a north-south direction.

Summary

Maps tell you about people and places in the world. The globe is a map of the Earth, and is the same shape as the Earth itself. Flat maps of the Earth, or part of it, are often collected together in an atlas.

The size, shape, or area of features on the Earth may be distorted when they are projected onto a flat map. On both globes and flat maps, lines of latitude and longitude help you to find the location of places.

All maps have a title and a legend to help you read the map. These tell you what the map is about, and what the symbols and colours used on the map represent. All maps also have a scale.

Geographic Terms

This is a view of an area that includes the main features found on the Earth's surface.

PEAK
MOUNTAINS
PASS
DIVIDE
SLOPE
VALLEY
PENINSULA
River
Coastline
Stream
HILL
Delta
Lake
LOWLANDS
Inlet
Bay
Gulf
Stream
FOOTHILLS
Tributary
Town
Railway
Cape
Archipelago
Strait
River
Road
CITY
Lagoon
Bridge
Road
Harbour
Bridge
BASIN
Reef
Canal
Town
Highway
Swamp
PLAIN
Creek
River Mouth
Village
Airport
Beach
Isthmus
Bay
Gulf
Cape
Lighthouse
Rocks
Bluff
Strait
Headland
SEA
Rocks
ISLAND

Mountains

Foothills

Lowlands

A map of the view shown on the opposite page would look like this.

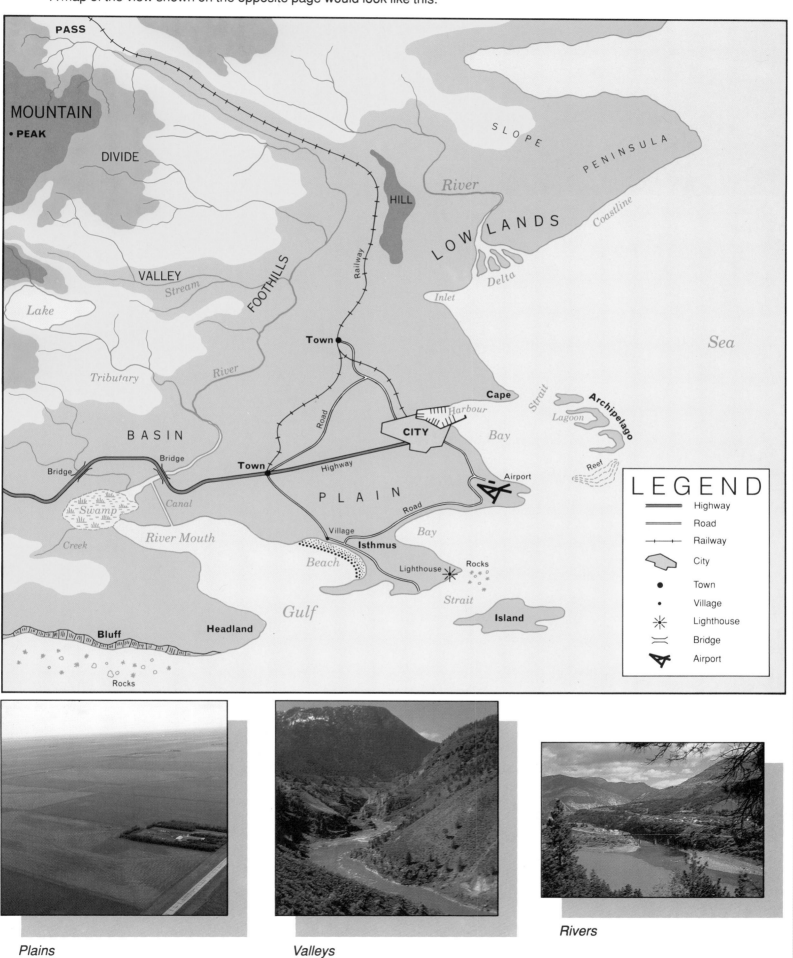

PASS

MOUNTAIN

• PEAK

DIVIDE

VALLEY

Lake

Stream

FOOTHILLS

Tributary

River

BASIN

Bridge

Bridge

Canal

Swamp

Creek

River Mouth

Town

Town

Highway

Road

PLAIN

Village

Isthmus

Beach

Gulf

Bluff

Headland

Rocks

Railway

HILL

River

SLOPE

PENINSULA

LOWLANDS

Coastline

Delta

Inlet

Sea

Harbour

Cape

Strait

Lagoon

Archipelago

CITY

Bay

Reef

Airport

Road

Bay

Lighthouse

Rocks

Strait

Island

LEGEND

═══	Highway
───	Road
╫╫╫	Railway
⬠	City
●	Town
•	Village
✳	Lighthouse
)(	Bridge
⊼	Airport

Plains

Valleys

Rivers

The World
POLITICAL DIVISIONS

Japan

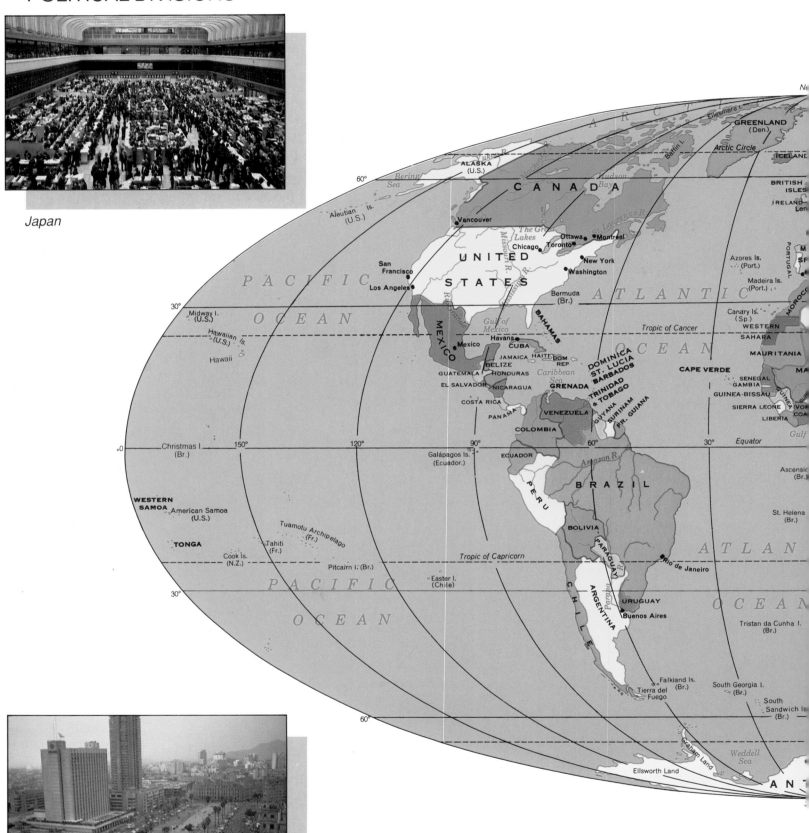

Peru

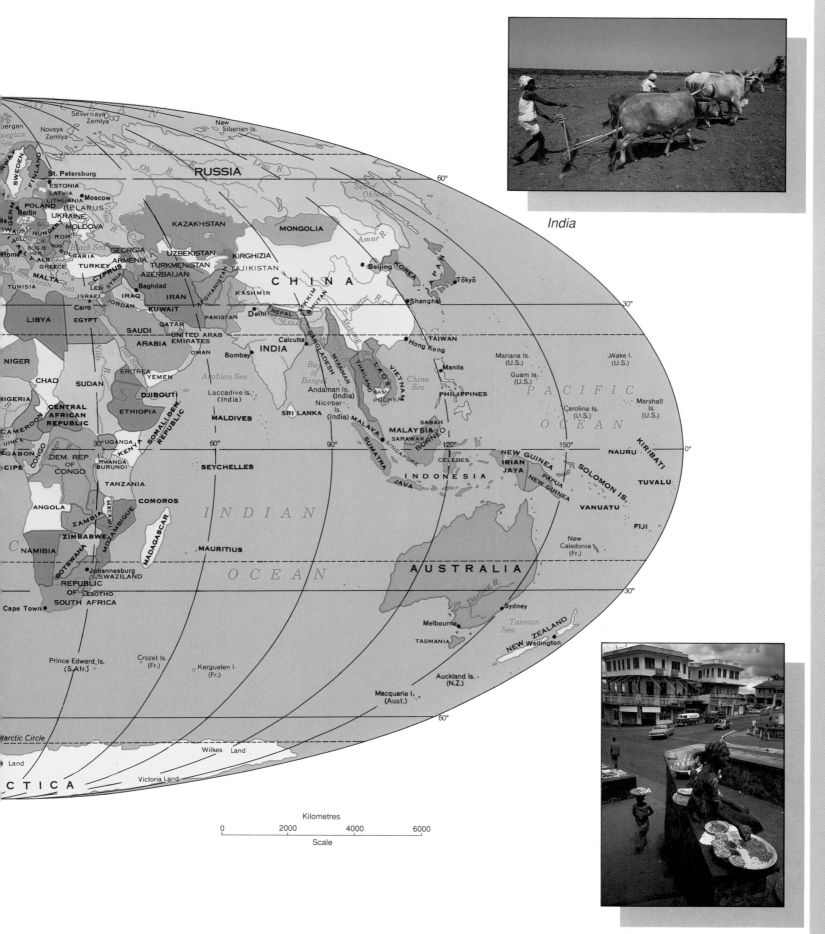

India

Ghana

OCEAN

Severnaya
Novaya   Zemlya
Spergen   Zemlya   New
Norwegian   Siberian Is.
Sea   60°
KWAIT   SWEDEN
FINLAND
St. Petersburg   Sea of
ESTONIA   Moscow   RUSSIA   Okhotsk
LATVIA
LITHUANIA
POLAND   BELARUS   KAZAKHSTAN   MONGOLIA   Amur R.
Berlin   UKRAINE
GERM   HUNG   MOLDOVA   JAPAN
AUS   SLOV   ROM   Black Sea   GEORGIA   UZBEKISTAN   KIRGHIZIA   Beijing   KOREA
BOS &   YUG   BULGARIA   ARMENIA   TURKMENISTAN   TAJIKISTAN   CHINA   Tōkyō
Rome   HER   GREECE   TURKEY   AZERBAIJAN   Shanghai   30°
MALTA   CYPRUS   LEB   SYRIA   AFGHANISTAN   KASHMIR   Yangtze R.
Mediterranean   ISRAEL   IRAQ   IRAN   TAIWAN
Sea   JORDAN   KUWAIT   PAKISTAN   Delhi   NEPAL   SIKKIM   BHUTAN   Hong Kong
TUNISIA   Cairo   QATAR   BANGLADESH   Mariana Is.   Wake I.
LIBYA   EGYPT   SAUDI   UNITED ARAB   Calcutta   MYANMAR   Manila   (U.S.)   (U.S.)
ARABIA   EMIRATES   Bombay   INDIA   LAOS   VIETNAM   PACIFIC
NIGER   OMAN   THAILAND   NAM   PHILIPPINES   Guam Is.   Marshall
CHAD   SUDAN   ERITREA   YEMEN   Arabian Sea   Bay   Andaman Is.   PUCHEA   (U.S.)   Is.
NIGERIA   DJIBOUTI   Laccadive Is.   of   (India)   China   OCEAN   (U.S.)
CENTRAL   (India)   Bengal   Nicobar   Sea   Caroline Is.
AFRICAN   ETHIOPIA   SOMALI DEM.   SRI LANKA   Is.   SABAH   (U.S.)
CAMEROON   REPUBLIC   REPUBLIC   MALDIVES   (India)   MALAYA   MALAYSIA
GUINEA   UGANDA   30°   60°   90°   SARAWAK   BORNEO   120°   NAURU   KIRIBATI   0°
GABON   CONGO   KENYA   SUMATRA   SINGAPORE   CELEBES   NEW GUINEA   150°   TUVALU
CIPE   DEM. REP.   RWANDA   SEYCHELLES   IRIAN   PAPUA   SOLOMON IS.
OF   BURUNDI   INDONESIA   JAVA   JAYA   NEW GUINEA
CONGO   TANZANIA   VANUATU
ANGOLA   COMOROS   INDIAN   FIJI
ZAMBIA   MALAWI   New
ZIMBABWE   MOZAMBIQUE   MADAGASCAR   MAURITIUS   AUSTRALIA   Caledonia
NAMIBIA   BOTSWANA   (Fr.)
OCEAN   Darling R.   30°
Johannesburg   SWAZILAND
REPUBLIC   LESOTHO   Sydney
OF   SOUTH AFRICA   Melbourne   Tasman
Cape Town   MAURITIUS   TASMANIA   Sea   NEW ZEALAND
Prince Edward Is.   Crozet Is.   Kerguelen I.   Wellington
(S.Afr.)   (Fr.)   (Fr.)
Auckland Is.
(N.Z.)
Macquarie I.   60°
(Aust.)
Antarctic Circle
Wilkes   Land
CTICA   Victoria Land

Kilometres
0   2000   4000   6000
Scale

The World
LANDFORMS–Relief

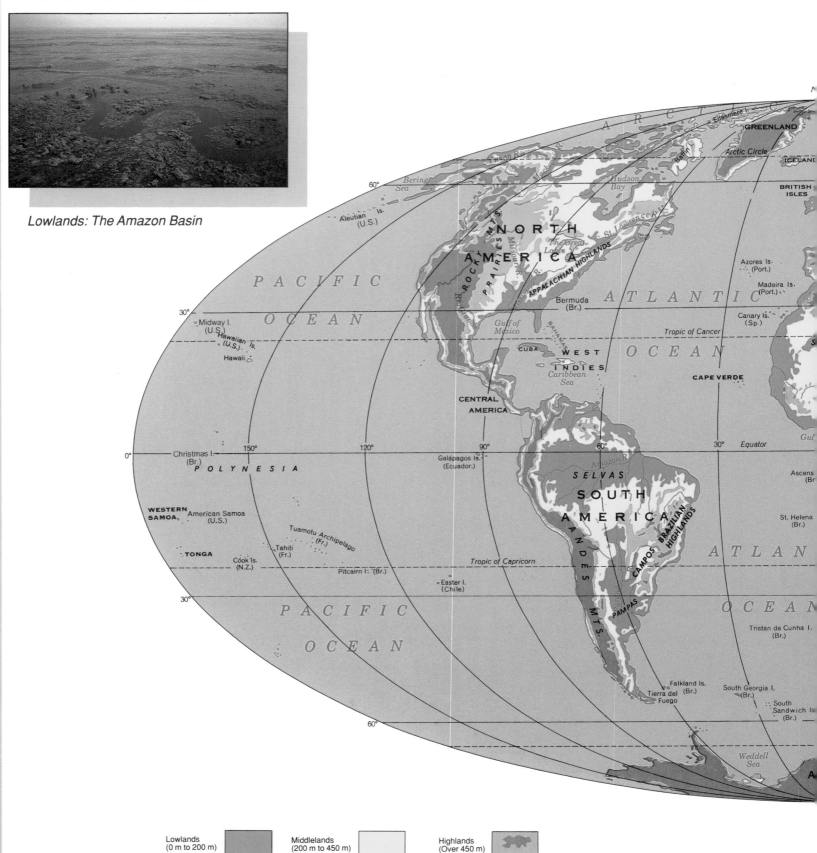

Lowlands: The Amazon Basin

ARCTIC

GREENLAND

Ellesmere I.

Arctic Circle

ICELAND

Baffin

Yukon R.

Hudson
Bay

BRITISH
ISLES

Bering
Sea

Aleutian Is.
(U.S.)

60°

NORTH
AMERICA

The Great
Lakes

St. Lawrence R.

ROCKY MTS.

PRAIRIES

APPALACHIAN HIGHLANDS

Azores Is.
(Port.)

PACIFIC

Missouri R.

Mississippi R.

Madeira Is.
(Port.)

OCEAN

Gulf of
Mexico

Bermuda
(Br.)

ATLANTIC

Canary Is.
(Sp.)

30°

Midway I.
(U.S.)

Hawaiian Is.
(U.S.)

Tropic of Cancer

OCEAN

Hawaii

CUBA

WEST
INDIES

BAHAMAS

CAPE VERDE

Caribbean
Sea

Christmas I.
(Br.)

CENTRAL
AMERICA

Galápagos Is.
(Ecuador.)

Amazon R.

SELVAS

Equator

30°

Gul

0°

150°

120°

90°

60°

POLYNESIA

SOUTH
AMERICA

Ascens
(Br

WESTERN
SAMOA

American Samoa
(U.S.)

ANDES MTS.

BRAZILIAN HIGHLANDS

CAMPOS

St. Helena
(Br.)

Tuamotu Archipelago
(Fr.)

ATLAN

TONGA

Tahiti
(Fr.)

Tropic of Capricorn

Cook Is.
(N.Z.)

Pitcairn I. (Br.)

Easter I.
(Chile)

PAMPAS

OCEAN

30°

PACIFIC

Tristan da Cunha I.
(Br.)

OCEAN

Falkland Is.
(Br.)

South Georgia I.
(Br.)

Tierra del
Fuego

South
Sandwich Is.
(Br.)

60°

Weddell
Sea

A

Lowlands (0 m to 200 m)	Middlelands (200 m to 450 m)	Highlands (Over 450 m)

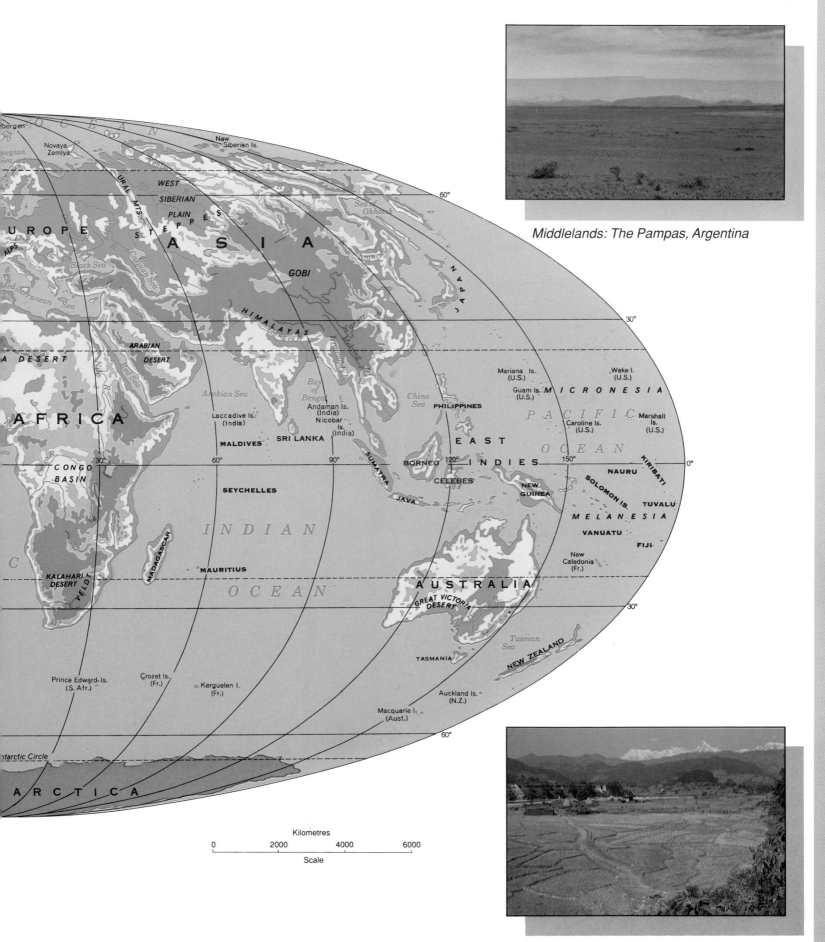

Middlelands: The Pampas, Argentina

Highlands: The Himalayas, Nepal

The World
VEGETATION

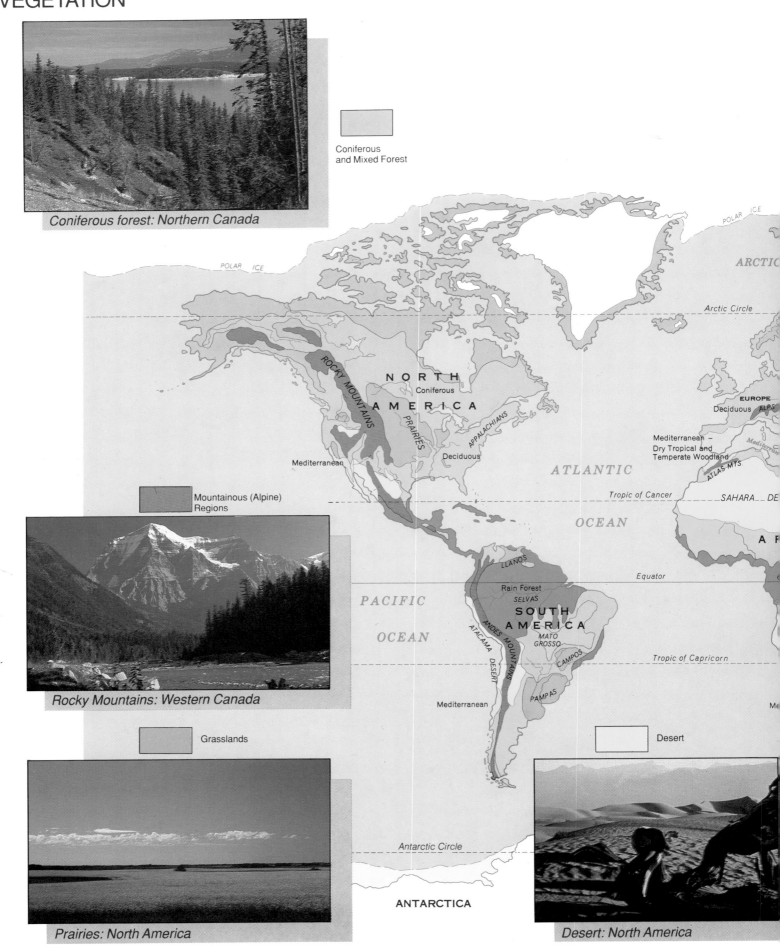

Coniferous forest: Northern Canada

Coniferous
and Mixed Forest

Mountainous (Alpine)
Regions

Rocky Mountains: Western Canada

Grasslands

Prairies: North America

Desert

Desert: North America

POLAR ICE

POLAR ICE

ARCTIC

Arctic Circle

NORTH
AMERICA

Coniferous

ROCKY MOUNTAINS

PRAIRIES

APPALACHIANS

Deciduous

Mediterranean

EUROPE
Deciduous ALPS

Mediterranean –
Dry Tropical and
Temperate Woodland

ATLAS MTS.

ATLANTIC

Tropic of Cancer

SAHARA DE

OCEAN

A

PACIFIC

OCEAN

LLANOS

Rain Forest
SELVAS

SOUTH
AMERICA

MATO
GROSSO

CAMPOS

ATACAMA
DESERT

ANDES MOUNTAINS

Equator

Tropic of Capricorn

PAMPAS

Mediterranean

Me

Antarctic Circle

ANTARCTICA

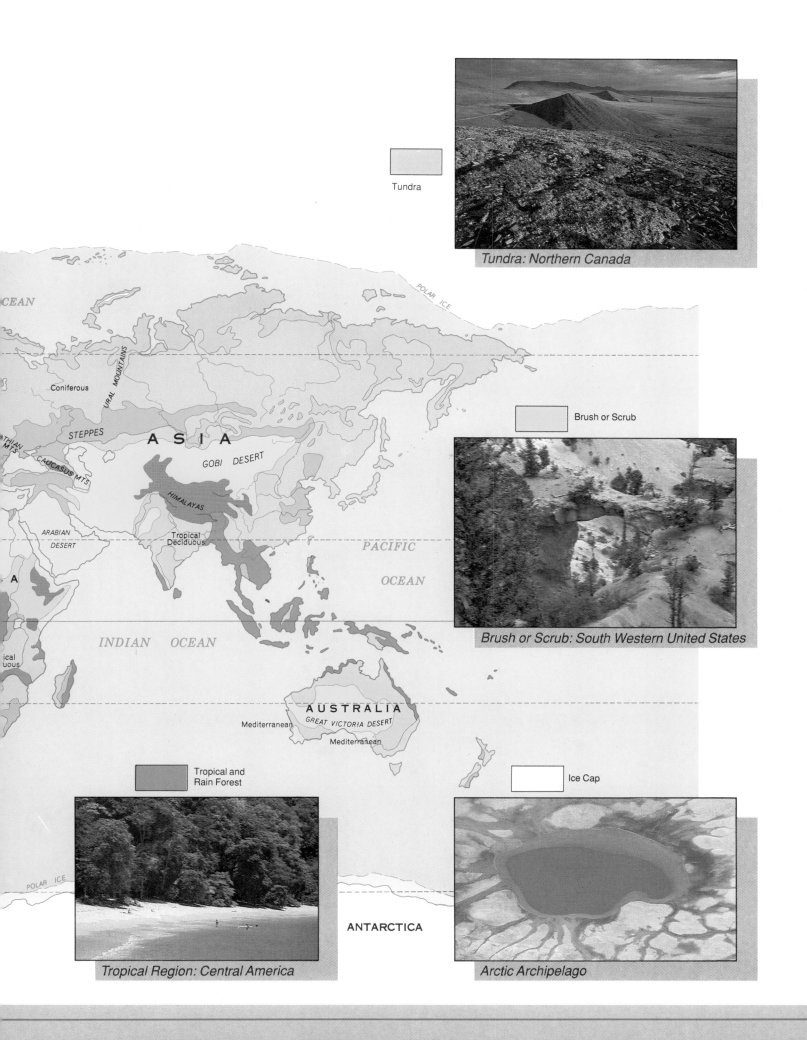

Tundra

Tundra: Northern Canada

POLAR ICE

Coniferous

URAL MOUNTAINS

STEPPES

CAUCASUS MTS

THIAN MTS

A S I A

GOBI DESERT

HIMALAYAS

ARABIAN DESERT

Tropical Deciduous

PACIFIC

OCEAN

Brush or Scrub

Brush or Scrub: South Western United States

INDIAN OCEAN

ical uous

AUSTRALIA

GREAT VICTORIA DESERT

Mediterranean

Mediterranean

Tropical and Rain Forest

Ice Cap

POLAR ICE

Tropical Region: Central America

ANTARCTICA

Arctic Archipelago

The World
HEMISPHERES

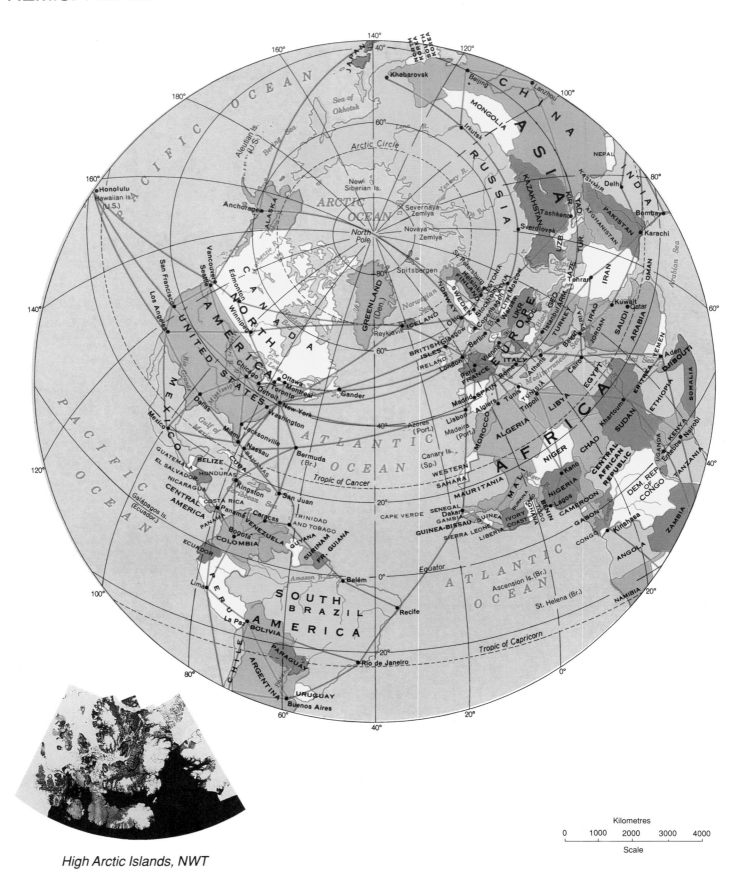

High Arctic Islands, NWT

Kilometres
0   1000   2000   3000   4000

Scale

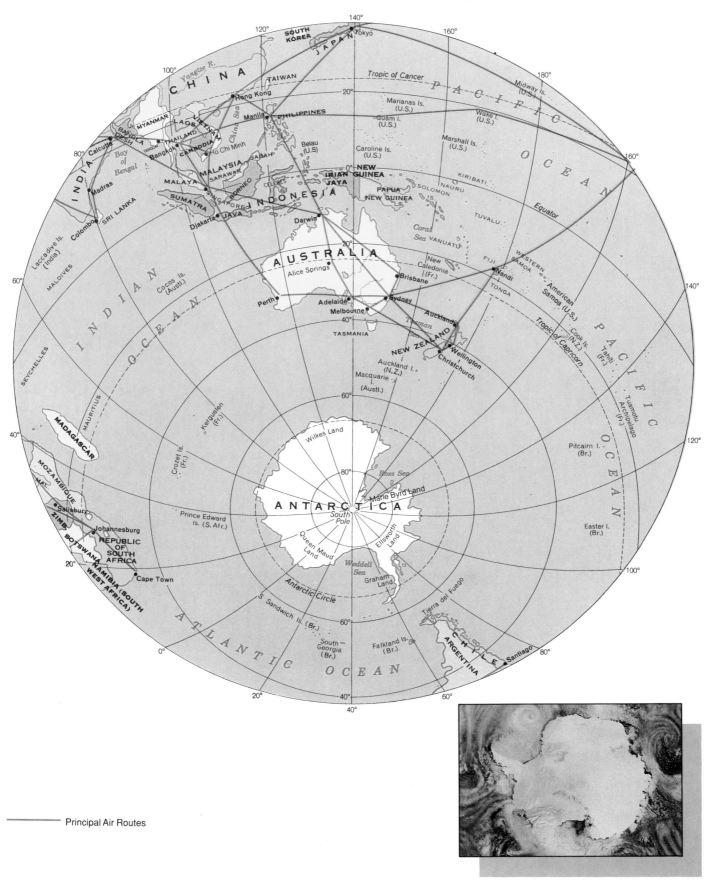

Principal Air Routes

Antarctica

North America
POLITICAL DIVISIONS

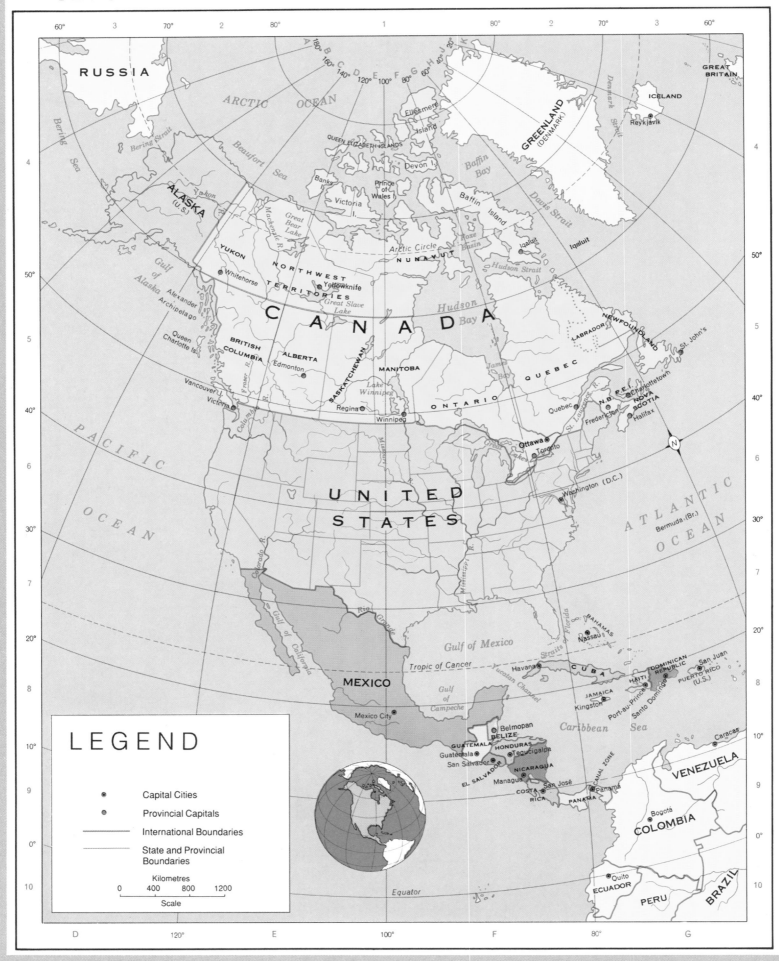

RUSSIA

ARCTIC OCEAN

Bering Sea

Bering Strait

ALASKA (U.S.)

Beaufort Sea

Banks

Victoria I.

Great Bear Lake

Yukon

Mackenzie R.

YUKON

Whitehorse

NORTHWEST TERRITORIES

Yellowknife

Great Slave Lake

Prince of Wales I.

QUEEN ELIZABETH ISLANDS

Devon I.

Ellesmere Island

Baffin Bay

Baffin Island

Arctic Circle

NUNAVUT

Foxe Basin

Hudson Strait

Iqaluit

Iqaluit

GREENLAND (DENMARK)

Denmark Strait

ICELAND

Reykjavik

GREAT BRITAIN

CANADA

Hudson Bay

LABRADOR

NEWFOUNDLAND

St. John's

Alexander Archipelago

Gulf of Alaska

Queen Charlotte Is.

BRITISH COLUMBIA

Fraser R.

ALBERTA

Edmonton

SASKATCHEWAN

MANITOBA

Lake Winnipeg

James Bay

ONTARIO

QUEBEC

St. Lawrence R.

Quebec

Frederic

N.B.

P.E.I.

Charlottetown

NOVA SCOTIA

Halifax

Vancouver I.

Victoria

Columbia R.

Regina

Winnipeg

Missouri R.

Great Lakes

Ottawa

Toronto

N

PACIFIC OCEAN

UNITED STATES

Washington (D.C.)

ATLANTIC OCEAN

Bermuda (Br.)

Colorado R.

Rio Grande

Gulf of California

Tropic of Cancer

Gulf of Mexico

Mississippi R.

Straits of Florida

BAHAMAS

Nassau

MEXICO

Gulf of Campeche

Yucatan Channel

Havana

CUBA

JAMAICA

Kingston

HAITI

Port-au-Prince

DOMINICAN REPUBLIC

Santo Domingo

San Juan

PUERTO RICO (U.S.)

Caribbean Sea

Mexico City

Belmopan

BELIZE

GUATEMALA

Guatemala

San Salvador

EL SALVADOR

HONDURAS

Tegucigalpa

NICARAGUA

Managua

COSTA RICA

San José

PANAMA

Panama

CANAL ZONE

Caracas

VENEZUELA

Bogotá

COLOMBIA

Quito

ECUADOR

PERU

BRAZIL

Equator

LEGEND

- ● Capital Cities
- ● Provincial Capitals
- — International Boundaries
- — State and Provincial Boundaries

Kilometres

0   400   800   1200

Scale

Parliament Buildings, Ottawa

The White House, Washington

Legislative Buildings, Mexico City

North America
LANDFORMS

LEGEND

Lowlands
(0 m to 200 m)

Middlelands
(200 m to 450 m)

Highlands
(Over 450 m)

Kilometres

0   400   800   1200

Scale

Gila monster—hot desert animal

Polar bears—cold desert animals

Tundra muskox

Swampland alligator

Grizzly bear—Western North American forest animal

North America
WINTER TEMPERATURES–January Averages

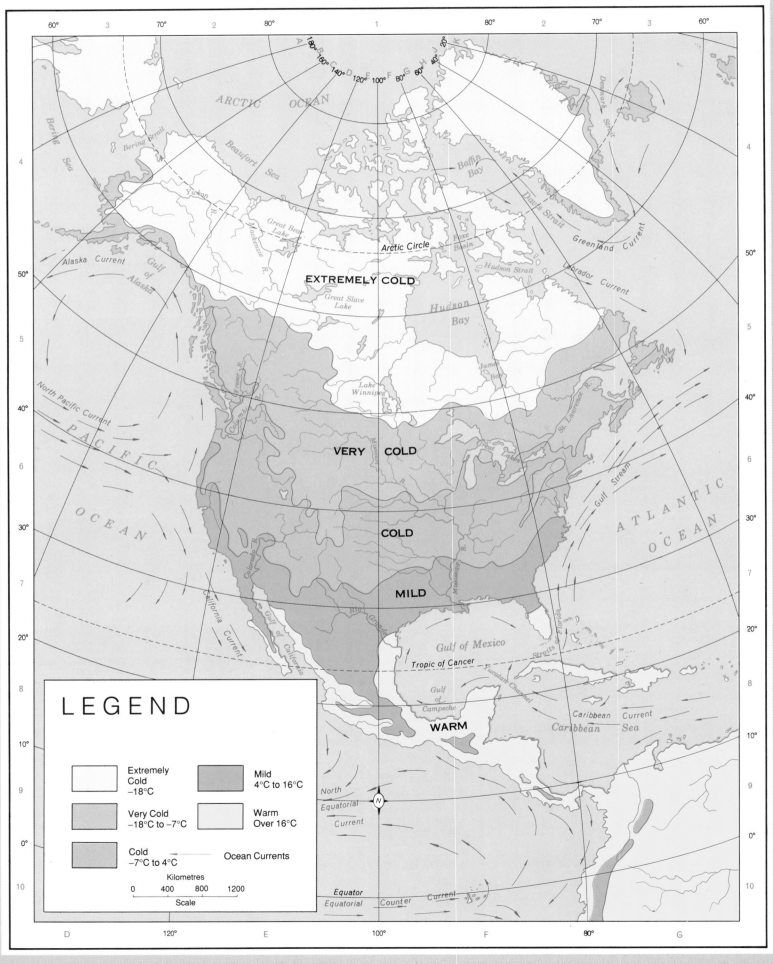

EXTREMELY COLD

VERY COLD

COLD

MILD

WARM

ARCTIC OCEAN

PACIFIC OCEAN

ATLANTIC OCEAN

Bering Sea

Bering Strait

Beaufort Sea

Baffin Bay

Denmark Strait

Yukon R.

Mackenzie R.

Great Bear Lake

Arctic Circle

Davis Strait

Greenland Current

Alaska Current

Gulf of Alaska

Great Slave Lake

Foxe Basin

Hudson Strait

Labrador Current

Hudson Bay

North Pacific Current

Fraser R.

Columbia R.

Lake Winnipeg

James Bay

St. Lawrence R.

Missouri R.

Great Lakes

Gulf Stream

Colorado R.

Mississippi R.

California Current

Gulf of California

Rio Grande

Gulf of Mexico

Tropic of Cancer

Straits of Florida

Yucatan Channel

Gulf of Campeche

Caribbean Current

Caribbean Sea

North Equatorial Current

Equator

Equatorial Counter Current

LEGEND

Extremely Cold −18°C	Mild 4°C to 16°C
Very Cold −18°C to −7°C	Warm Over 16°C
Cold −7°C to 4°C	Ocean Currents

Kilometres

0   400   800   1200

Scale

North America
SUMMER TEMPERATURES–July Averages

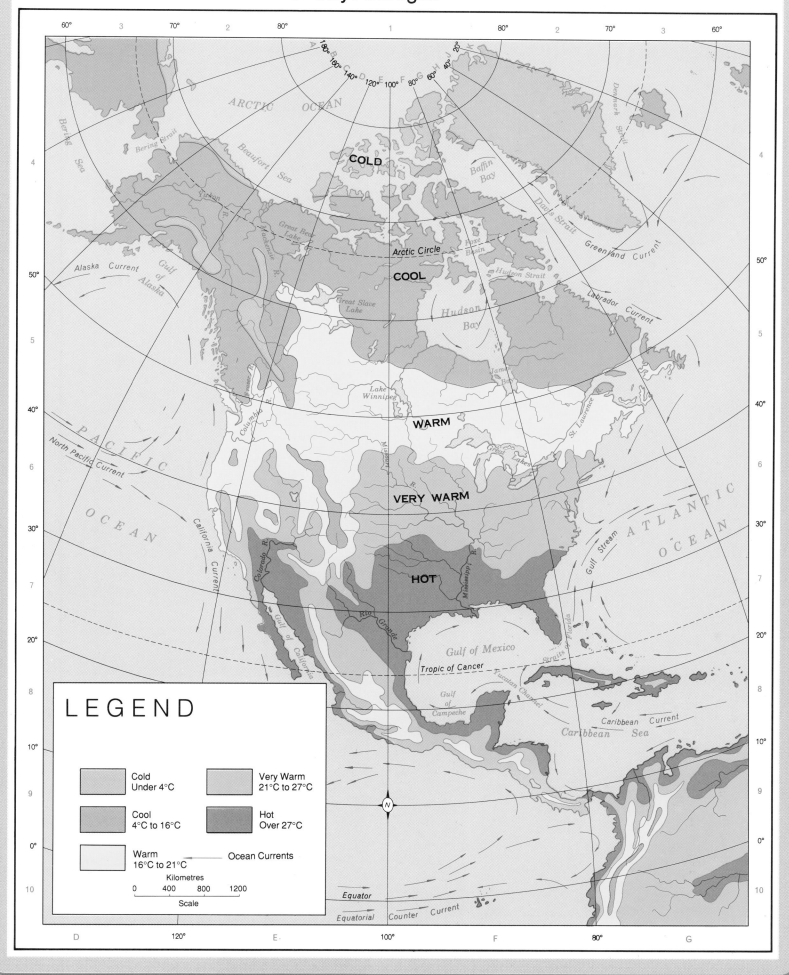

LEGEND

Cold
Under 4°C

Cool
4°C to 16°C

Warm
16°C to 21°C

Very Warm
21°C to 27°C

Hot
Over 27°C

Ocean Currents

Kilometres

0   400   800   1200

Scale

North America
AVERAGE ANNUAL RAINFALL

LEGEND

Very Light 0 mm to 250 mm	Heavy 1000 mm to 1500 mm
Light 250 mm to 500 mm	Very Heavy Over 1500 mm
Moderate 500 mm to 1000 mm	Prevailing Winds

Kilometres
0   400   800   1200
Scale

North America
VEGETATION and LAND USE

LEGEND

Mainly Ice-Covered Areas	Swampland, Marshland
Tundra	Forested Areas
Grasslands	Areas of Intensive Farming
Mainly Desert	Irrigated Areas

Livestock Grazing

Kilometres
0   400   800   1200
Scale

Canada
POLITICAL DIVISIONS

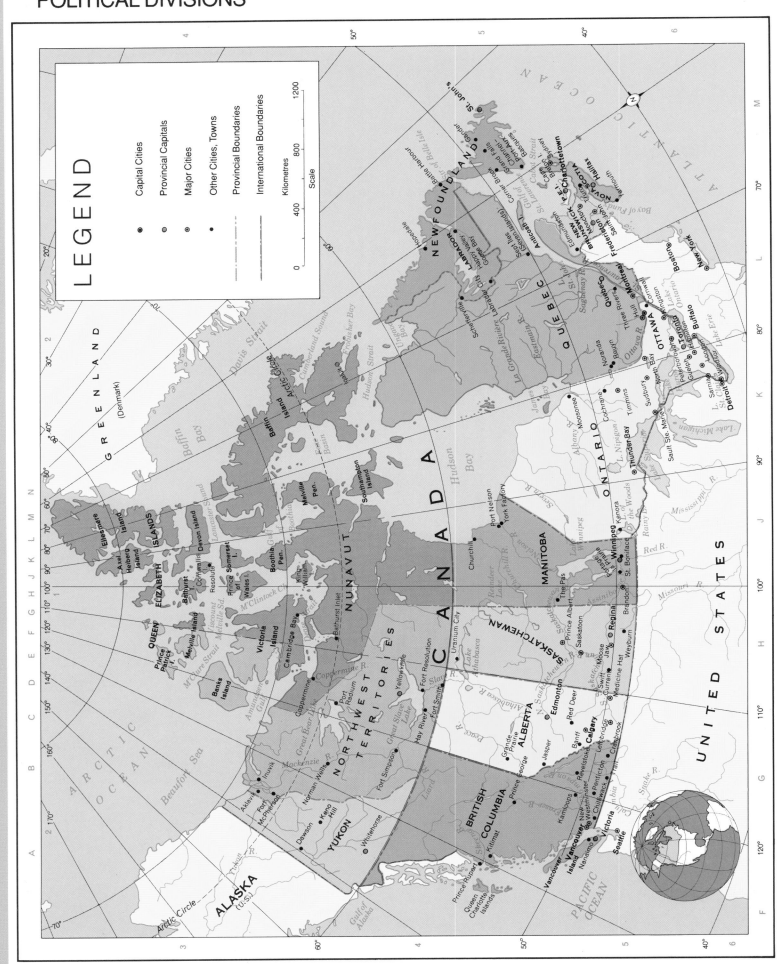

LEGEND

- Capital Cities
- Provincial Capitals
- Major Cities
- Other Cities, Towns
- Provincial Boundaries
- International Boundaries

Scale

Kilometres

0   400   800   1200

Population of the Capital Cities of Canada

City	City Core	Metropolitan Area
St. John's	101 936	174 051
Halifax	113 910	322 518
Charlottetown	32 531	
Fredericton	46 507	
Quebec	167 264	671 889
Toronto	653 734	4 263 757
Winnipeg	618 447	667 209
Regina	180 400	193 652
Edmonton	616 306	852 597
Victoria	73 504	304 287
Whitehorse	19 157	
Yellowknife	17 275	
Iqaluit	3 600	

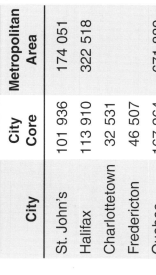

Quebec City, PQ

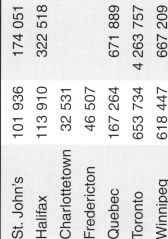

Regina, SK

St. John's, NF

Charlottetown, PE

Toronto, ON

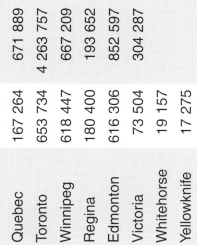

Iqaluit, Nunavut

Halifax, NS

Yellowknife, NWT

Edmonton, AB

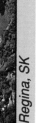

Winnipeg, MB

Victoria, BC

Whitehorse, YT

Fredericton, NB

Canada
LANDFORMS–Relief

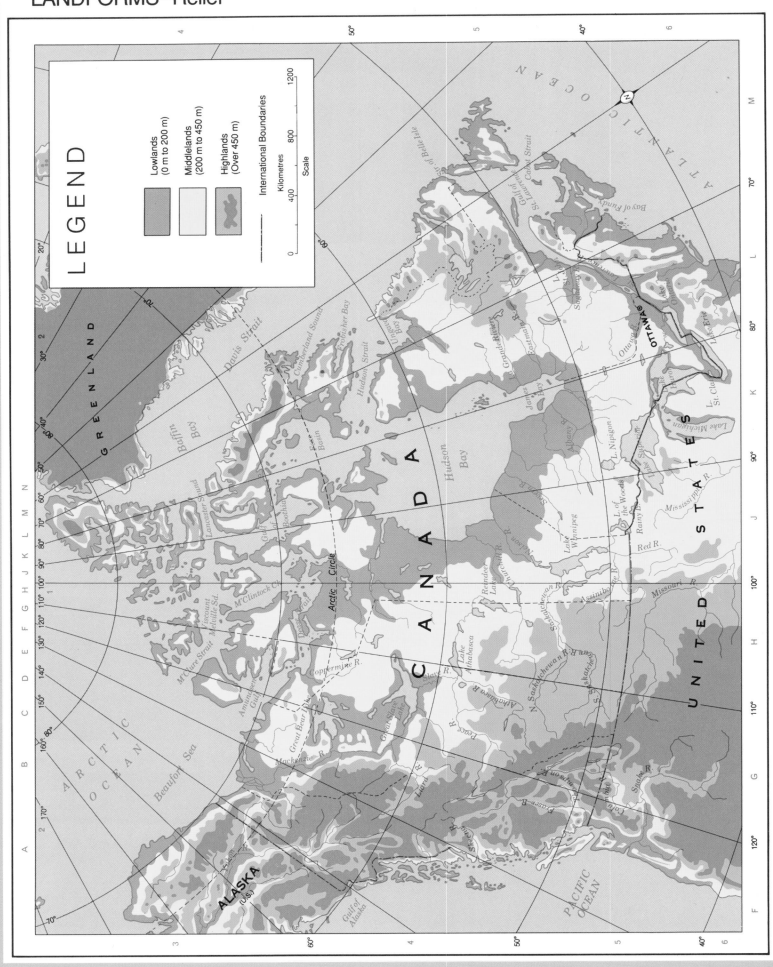

LEGEND

Lowlands (0 m to 200 m)
Middlelands (200 m to 450 m)
Highlands (Over 450 m)
International Boundaries

Scale
Kilometres
0   400   800   1200

Deciduous forest in the fall, ON

Prairie grasslands, AB

Old growth forest, BC

Canada
VEGETATION and LAND–SURFACE REGIONS

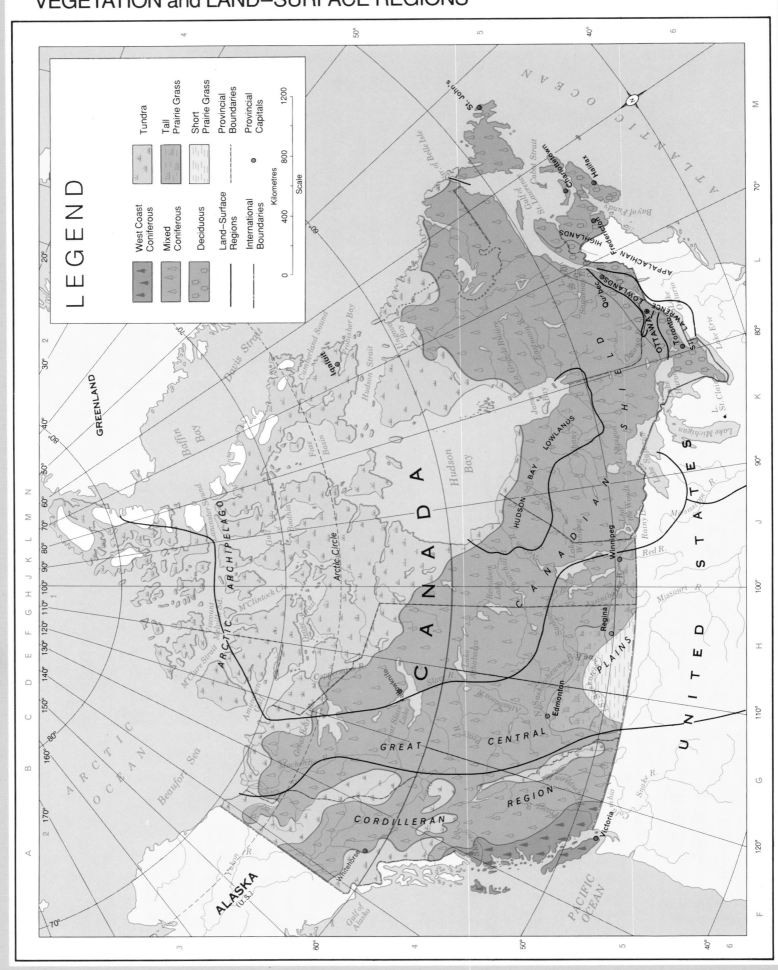

LEGEND

West Coast Coniferous
Mixed Coniferous
Deciduous

Tundra
Tall Prairie Grass
Short Prairie Grass

Land–Surface Regions
International Boundaries
Provincial Boundaries
Provincial Capitals

Scale

Kilometres
0   400   800   1200

Canada
SETTLED AREAS–Population

Canada
A MULTICULTURAL SOCIETY

Ukrainians in western Canada

Canadian students

Bonhomme in Quebec

National Backgrounds of Canadians
1996 Census

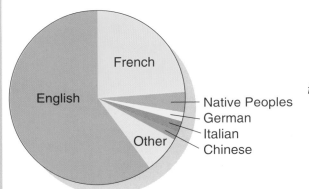

French

English

Native Peoples
German
Italian
Chinese

Other

Ovide Mercredi, former national Chief of the Assembly of First Nations, received the sacred bundle from elder during a swearing-in ceremony, June 12, 1991.

Immigration by Province

	Total Immigrants	NF	PE	NS	NB	PQ	ON	MB	SK	AB	BC	YT, NUN, NWT
1961	71 689	365	69	901	770	16 920	36 518	2 527	1 333	4 823	7 326	137
1966	194 743	805	141	2 084	1 283	39 198	107 621	5 132	3 440	10 078	24 746	215
1971	121 900	819	172	1 812	1 038	19 222	64 357	5 301	1 426	8 653	18 917	183
1976	149 429	725	235	1 942	1 752	29 282	72 031	5 509	2 323	14 896	20 484	250
1981	128 618	483	128	1 405	990	21 182	55 032	5 370	2 402	19 330	22 095	201
1986	99 219	274	168	1 097	641	19 459	49 630	3 749	1 860	9 673	12 552	116
1991	232 020	641	150	1 504	685	52 155	119 257	5 659	2 455	17 043	32 263	208
1996	226 074	584	153	3 221	715	29 671	119 681	3 923	1 823	13 893	52 025	179
1997	216 044	437	151	2 891	663	27 672	118 060	3 804	1 742	12 919	47 459	186*

*Preliminary Figures.
What do you think attracts newcomers to settle in your province?

East Indian woman displaying traditional cuisine

Kensington Market, Toronto

Caribana Parade in Toronto

Chinese Shopping District, Vancouver

Where do immigrants to Canada come from? (1996)

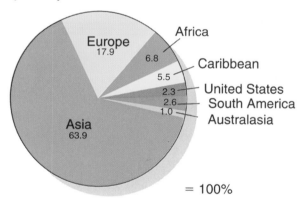

Europe 17.9
Africa 6.8
Caribbean 5.5
United States 2.3
South America 2.6
Australasia 1.0
Asia 63.9

= 100%

Immigration & Emigration to 1996

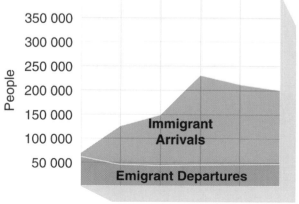

People

350 000
300 000
250 000
200 000
150 000
100 000
50 000

Immigrant Arrivals

Emigrant Departures

1961 1971 1981 1991 1993 1996

Where do refugees to Canada come from? (1996)

Asia	15 954
Africa	2 829
Eastern Europe	4 526
Central America	1 386
Australasia	237
Sourth America	361
Other	31

Total number of people = 25 324

Canada
LAKES and RIVERS

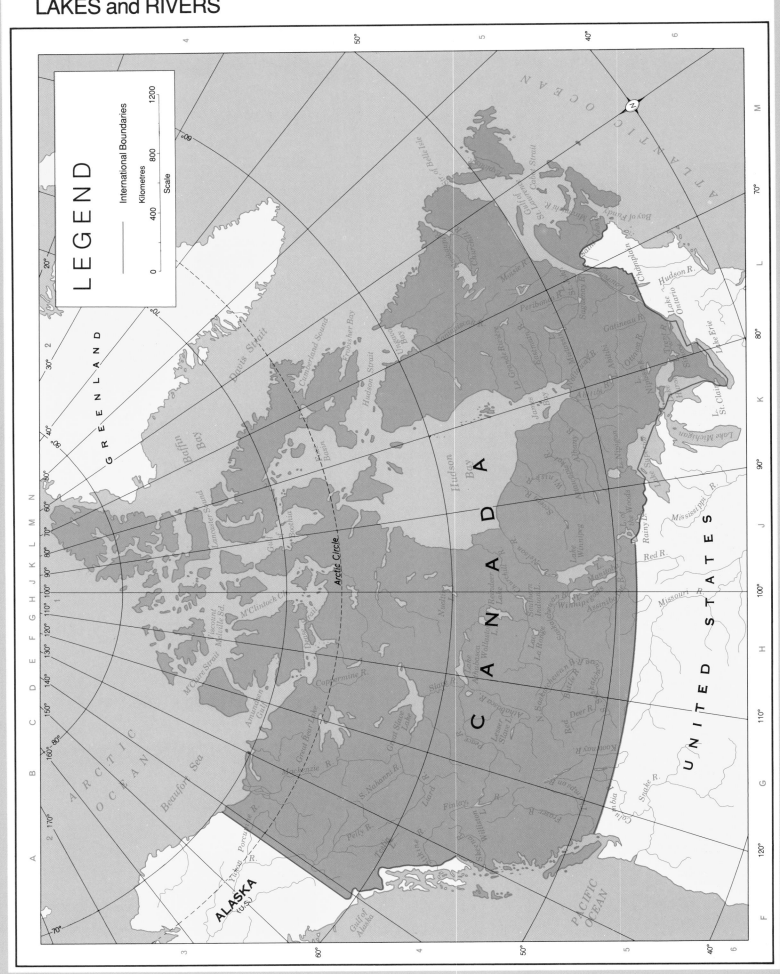

LEGEND

International Boundaries

Scale

Kilometres

0   400   800   1200

Canada
AIR TRANSPORTATION

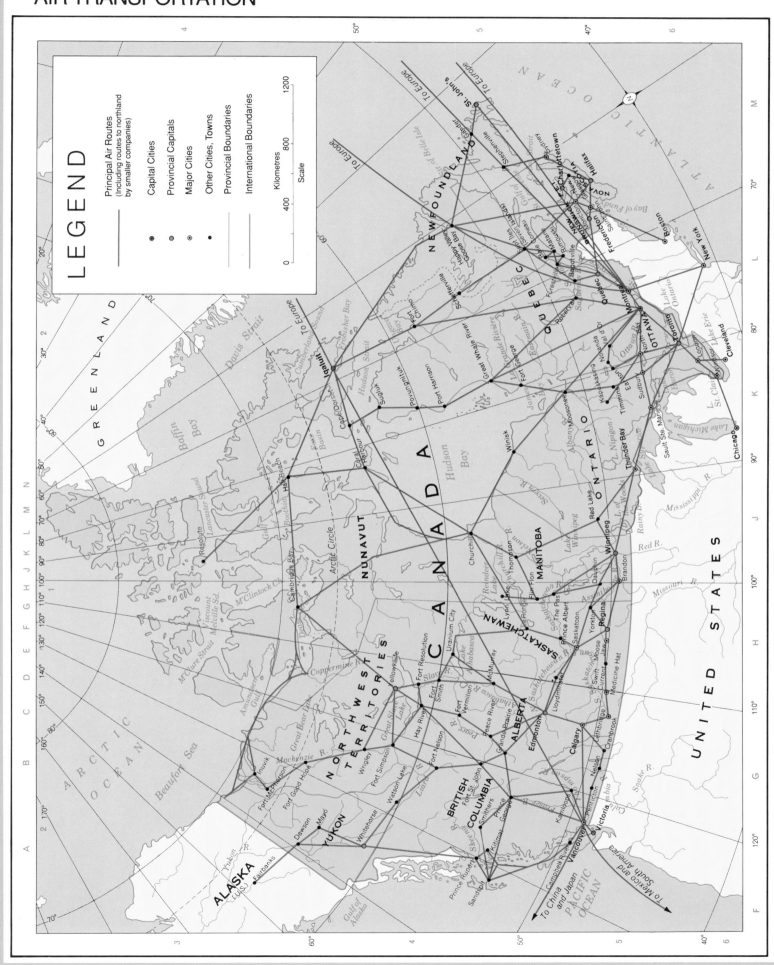

Canada
TRANSPORTATION

Competition and rising prices can affect transportation. Canadian railway companies have reorganized services and in some cases cancelled service on existing routes.

LEGEND

Principal Railways
Trans-Canada Highway
Capital Cities
Provincial Capitals
Major Cities
Other Cities, Towns
Provincial Boundaries
International Boundaries

Kilometres
0   400   800   1200
Scale

Canada
NATURAL RESOURCES

As natural resources are depleted or the demand for them declines, companies close existing mines and seek new sites.

Newfoundland
TRANSPORTATION

Competition and rising prices can affect transportation. Canadian railway companies have reorganized services and in some cases cancelled service on existing routes.

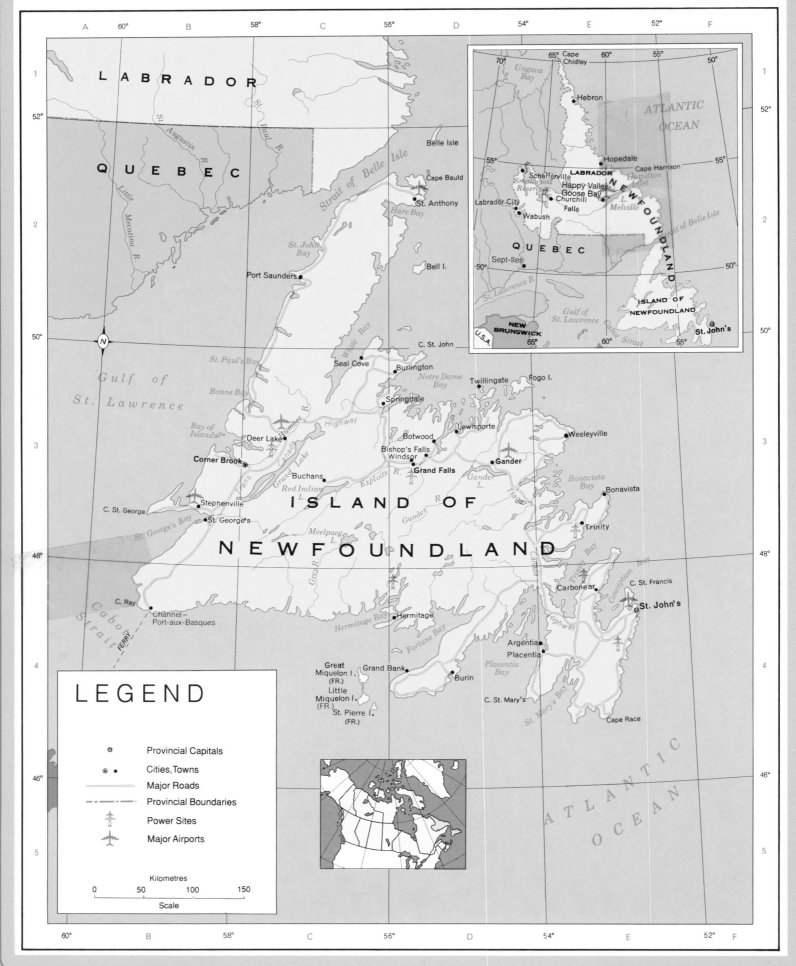

LABRADOR

QUEBEC

Belle Isle

Cape Bauld

St. Anthony

Strait of Belle Isle

Hare Bay

St. John Bay

Port Saunders

Bell I.

St. Paul's Bay

C. St. John

Seal Cove
Burlington

Notre Dame Bay

Twillingate
Fogo I.

Bonne Bay

Springdale

Gulf of St. Lawrence

Bay of Islands

Deer Lake

Botwood

Lewisporte

Wesleyville

Corner Brook

Bishop's Falls
Windsor

Gander

Buchans

Grand Falls

Red Indian L.

Bonavista Bay

Bonavista

ISLAND OF

Stephenville

C. St. George

Trinity

St. George's

Meelpaeg L.

NEWFOUNDLAND

C. St. Francis

Carbonear

Conception Bay

C. Ray

Hermitage

St. John's

Channel-Port-aux-Basques

Cabot Strait

FERRY

Hermitage Bay

Fortune Bay

Argentia
Placentia

Great Miquelon I. (FR.)

Grand Bank

Burin

Placentia Bay

Little Miquelon I. (FR.)

St. Pierre I. (FR.)

C. St. Mary's

St. Mary's Bay

Cape Race

ATLANTIC OCEAN

Inset map (Labrador)

Cape Chidley

Ungava Bay

Hebron

ATLANTIC OCEAN

Hopedale

Cape Harrison

Schefferville

LABRADOR

Hamilton Inlet

Happy Valley-Goose Bay

Smallwood Reservoir

Churchill Falls

L. Melville

NEWFOUNDLAND

Labrador City

Wabush

Strait of Belle Isle

QUEBEC

Sept-Iles

St. Lawrence R.

Gulf of St. Lawrence

ISLAND OF NEWFOUNDLAND

Cabot Strait

NEW BRUNSWICK

U.S.A.

St. John's

LEGEND

- ⊙ Provincial Capitals
- ⊙ • Cities, Towns
- Major Roads
- Provincial Boundaries
- Power Sites
- Major Airports

Kilometres

0   50   100   150

Scale

Newfoundland
LANDFORMS–Relief

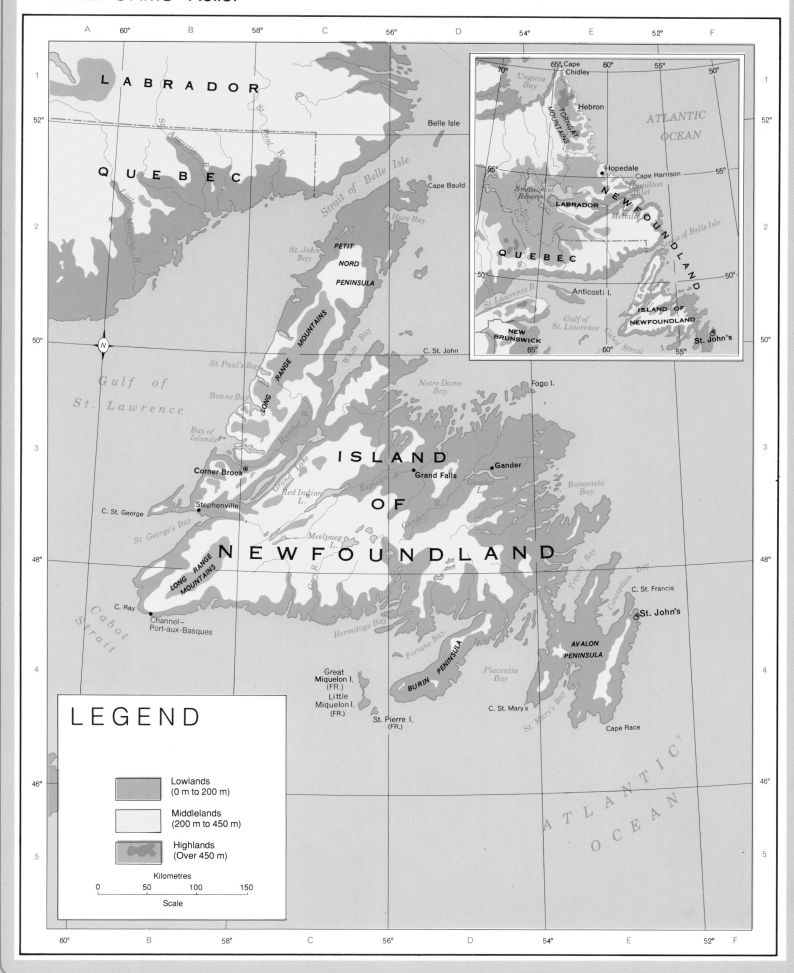

LEGEND

Lowlands
(0 m to 200 m)

Middlelands
(200 m to 450 m)

Highlands
(Over 450 m)

Kilometres

0   50   100   150

Scale

Newfoundland
VEGETATION and INDUSTRIES

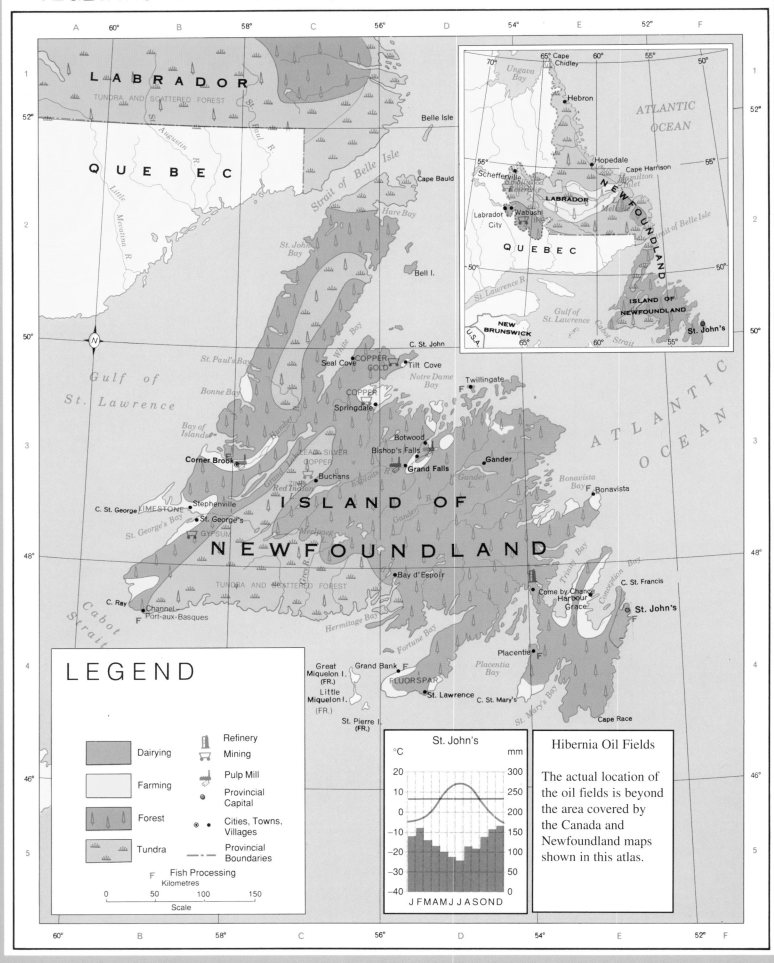

LABRADOR
TUNDRA AND SCATTERED FOREST

QUEBEC

Little Mecatina R.

St. Augustin R.

St. Paul R.

Belle Isle

Strait of Belle Isle

Cape Bauld

Hare Bay

St. John Bay

Bell I.

White Bay

C. St. John

Seal Cove   COPPER   Tilt Cove
GOLD
Notre Dame Bay
COPPER   Twillingate
Springdale   F

St. Paul's Bay

Gulf of
St. Lawrence

Bonne Bay

Bay of Islands

Humber R.

Botwood
Bishop's Falls
LEAD SILVER
COPPER   Grand Falls   Gander
Corner Brook
Buchans   Exploits R.   Gander L.
Red Indian L.

Bonavista Bay   F Bonavista

C. St. George LIMESTONE   Stephenville
St. George's
St. George's Bay   GYPSUM
Meelpaeg L.

ISLAND OF

NEWFOUNDLAND

Grey R.

Bay d'Espoir

Trinity Bay   C. St. Francis

Come by Chance
Harbour Grace
Conception Bay   St. John's

TUNDRA AND SCATTERED FOREST

C. Ray
Channel
Port-aux-Basques   F

Cabot Strait

Hermitage Bay

Fortune Bay

Placentia F

Placentia Bay

Great Miquelon I. (FR.)   Grand Bank F
Little Miquelon I. (FR.)   FLUORSPAR
St. Lawrence   C. St. Mary's
St. Pierre I. (FR.)

St. Mary's Bay

Cape Race

Inset map (Labrador)
Ungava Bay   65° Cape Chidley
Hebron
ATLANTIC OCEAN
Schefferville   Hopedale   Cape Harrison
Hamilton Inlet
Smallwood Reservoir   LABRADOR   NEWFOUNDLAND
Labrador City   Wabush   Melville L.
QUEBEC
St. Lawrence R.
NEW BRUNSWICK
U.S.A.
Gulf of St. Lawrence
Cabot Strait
ISLAND OF NEWFOUNDLAND
St. John's

ATLANTIC OCEAN

LEGEND

Dairying	⛴ Refinery
Farming	⛏ Mining
Forest	Pulp Mill
Tundra	⊙ Provincial Capital
	⦿ • Cities, Towns, Villages
	— ·· — Provincial Boundaries

F   Fish Processing

Kilometres
0   50   100   150
Scale

St. John's
°C   mm
20   300
10   250
0   200
-10   150
-20   100
-30   50
-40   0
J F M A M J J A S O N D

Hibernia Oil Fields

The actual location of the oil fields is beyond the area covered by the Canada and Newfoundland maps shown in this atlas.

Maritime Provinces
TRANSPORTATION

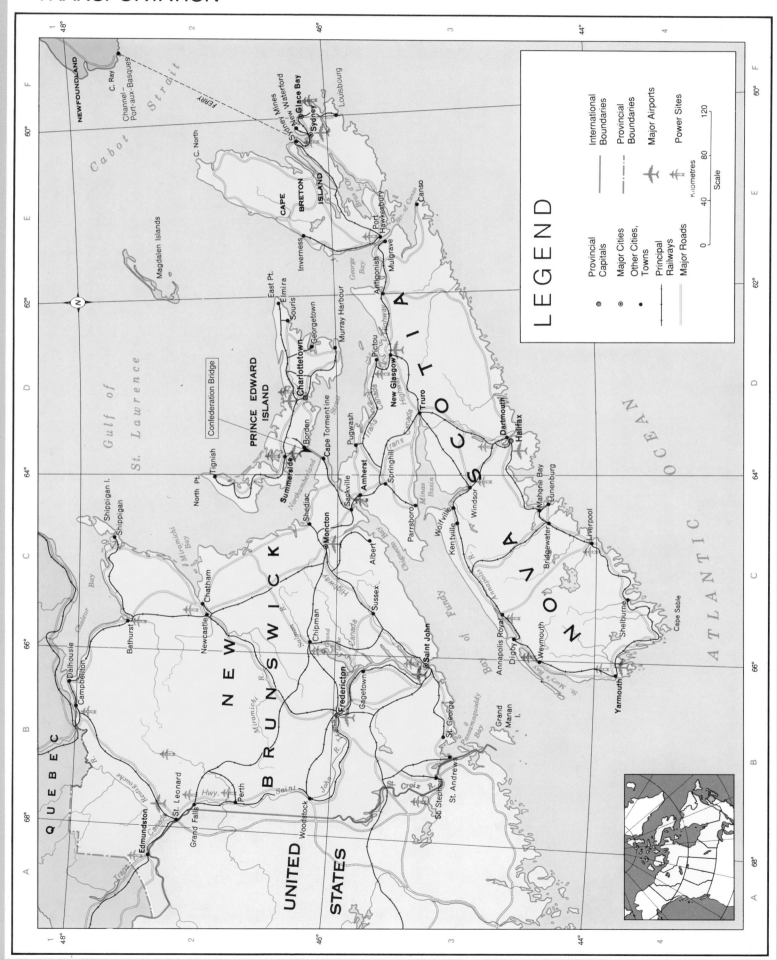

LEGEND

● Provincial Capitals	—— International Boundaries
◉ Major Cities	—·—·— Provincial Boundaries
• Other Cities, Towns	✈ Major Airports
╫ Principal Railways	✈ Power Sites
—— Major Roads	

Kilometres
0   40   80   120
Scale

QUEBEC

NEWFOUNDLAND

C. Ray
Channel–Port-aux-Basques
FERRY

Cabot Strait

Gulf of St. Lawrence

Magdalen Islands

C. North

East Pt.
Elmira
Souris

CAPE BRETON ISLAND

Sydney Mines
New Waterford
Glace Bay
Sydney
Louisbourg

Inverness

Canso

Port Hawkesbury
Mulgrave
Antigonish

George Bay

Str. of Canso

Bras d'Or L.

PRINCE EDWARD ISLAND

Tignish
Summerside
Charlottetown
Murray Harbour
Georgetown
Borden
Cape Tormentine

Confederation Bridge

Northumberland Strait

North Pt.

Pictou
New Glasgow
Pugwash
Truro
Dartmouth
Halifax

Trans Canada Highway

NOVA SCOTIA

Amherst
Springhill
Parrsboro
Sackville

Minas Basin

Wolfville
Kentville
Windsor
Mahone Bay
Lunenburg
Bridgewater
Liverpool
Shelburne

Cape Sable

NEW BRUNSWICK

Shippigan I.
Shippigan

Chaleur Bay

Bathurst
Dalhousie
Campbellton

Restigouche R.

Miramichi Bay

Chatham
Newcastle

Miramichi R.

Moncton
Shediac

Chipman
Albert
Sussex

Salmon R.

Nepisiguit R.

Bay of Fundy

St. Leonard
Perth
Grand Falls
Edmundston

Trans Canada Hwy.

Saint John R.

Woodstock

Fredericton
Gagetown

Saint John

St. Croix R.

St. George
St. Stephen
St. Andrews

Passamaquoddy Bay

Grand Manan I.

Annapolis Royal
Digby
Weymouth
Yarmouth

St. Mary's Bay

Annapolis R.

UNITED STATES

ATLANTIC OCEAN

N

Maritime Provinces
LANDFORMS–Relief

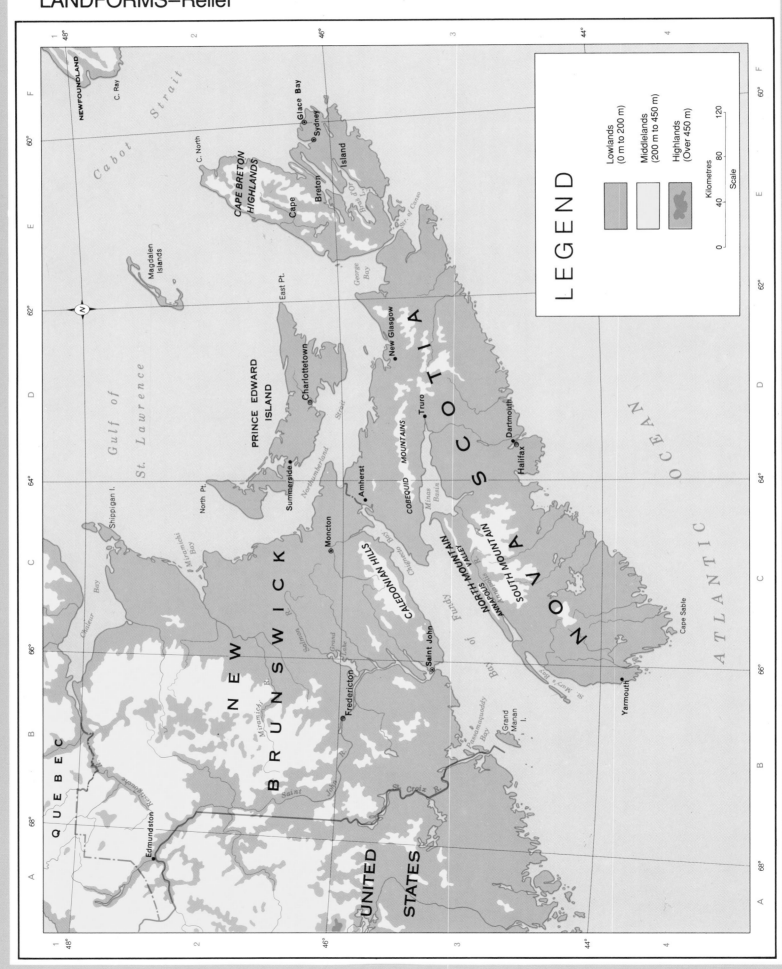

LEGEND

Lowlands (0 m to 200 m)

Middlelands (200 m to 450 m)

Highlands (Over 450 m)

Kilometres

0   40   80   120

Scale

NEWFOUNDLAND

C. Ray

Cabot Strait

C. North

CAPE BRETON HIGHLANDS

Cape Breton Island

Glace Bay

Sydney

Bras d'Or L.

Str. of Canso

George Bay

Magdalen Islands

East Pt.

Gulf of St. Lawrence

PRINCE EDWARD ISLAND

Charlottetown

Summerside

North Pt.

Northumberland Strait

New Glasgow

S C O T I A

Truro

COBEQUID MOUNTAINS

Minas Basin

Dartmouth

Halifax

N O V A

Shippigan I.

Miramichi Bay

Chaleur Bay

Amherst

Moncton

Chignecto Bay

NORTH MOUNTAIN

ANNAPOLIS VALLEY

SOUTH MOUNTAIN

O C E A N

N E W   B R U N S W I C K

Salmon R.

Grand Lake

CALEDONIAN HILLS

Saint John

Bay of Fundy

A T L A N T I C

Cape Sable

Miramichi R.

Fredericton

Saint John R.

St. Croix R.

St. Mary's Bay

Passamaquoddy Bay

Grand Manan I.

Yarmouth

Q U E B E C

Restigouche R.

Edmundston

UNITED STATES

Maritime Provinces
FARMING and FORESTRY

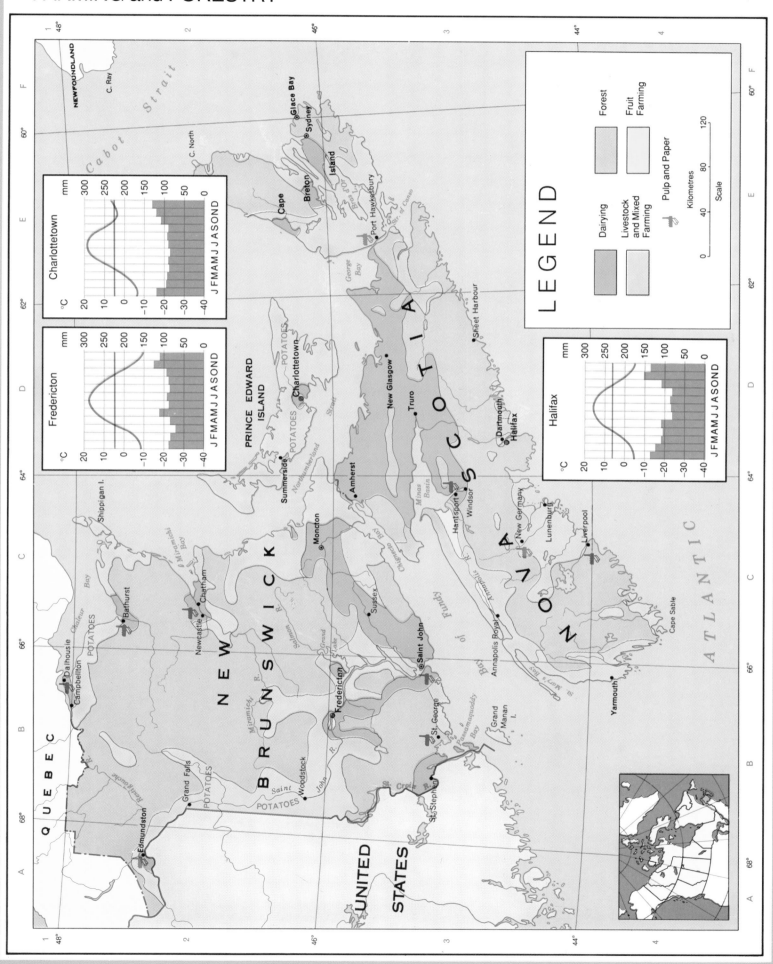

LEGEND

- Dairying
- Livestock and Mixed Farming
- Forest
- Fruit Farming
- Pulp and Paper

Kilometres
0 40 80 120
Scale

Charlottetown

mm
300
250
200
150
100
50
0

°C
20
10
0
-10
-20
-30
-40

J F M A M J J A S O N D

Fredericton

mm
300
250
200
150
100
50
0

°C
20
10
0
-10
-20
-30
-40

J F M A M J J A S O N D

Halifax

mm
300
250
200
150
100
50
0

°C
20
10
0
-10
-20
-30
-40

J F M A M J J A S O N D

NEWFOUNDLAND
C. Ray
Cabot Strait
C. North
Glace Bay
Sydney
Cape Breton Island
Bras d'Or
Port Hawkesbury
Str. of Canso
George Bay
Sheet Harbour
NOVA SCOTIA
New Glasgow
Truro
Dartmouth
Halifax
Amherst
Minas Basin
Hantsport
Windsor
Windsor R.
New Germany
Lunenburg
Liverpool
Annapolis R.
Annapolis Royal
Cape Sable
ATLANTIC
Yarmouth
St. Mary's Bay
Bay of Fundy
Chignecto Bay
PRINCE EDWARD ISLAND
POTATOES
Charlottetown
Summerside
POTATOES
Northumberland Strait
Sussex
Saint John
Fredericton
St. George
Grand Manan I.
Passamaquoddy Bay
St. Croix R.
St. Stephen
POTATOES
Woodstock
Saint John R.
Grand Lake
Salmon R.
NEW BRUNSWICK
Moncton
Newcastle
Chatham
Miramichi Bay
Bathurst
Chaleur Bay
Shippigan I.
POTATOES
Dalhousie
Campbellton
QUEBEC
Grand Falls
POTATOES
Rivière Restigouche
Edmundston
Miramichi R.
UNITED STATES
Bay of Fundy

Atlantic Provinces
MINING

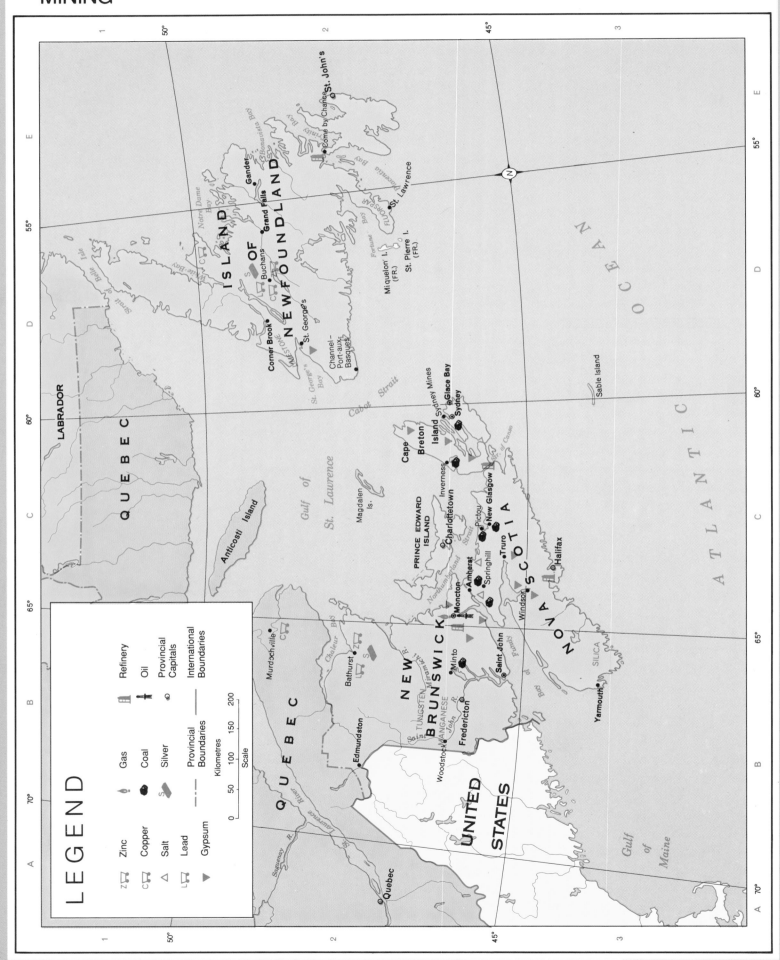

Atlantic Provinces

FISHING

For species, such as cod and salmon, the numbers have decreased so much that the government has imposed limitations on their catch.

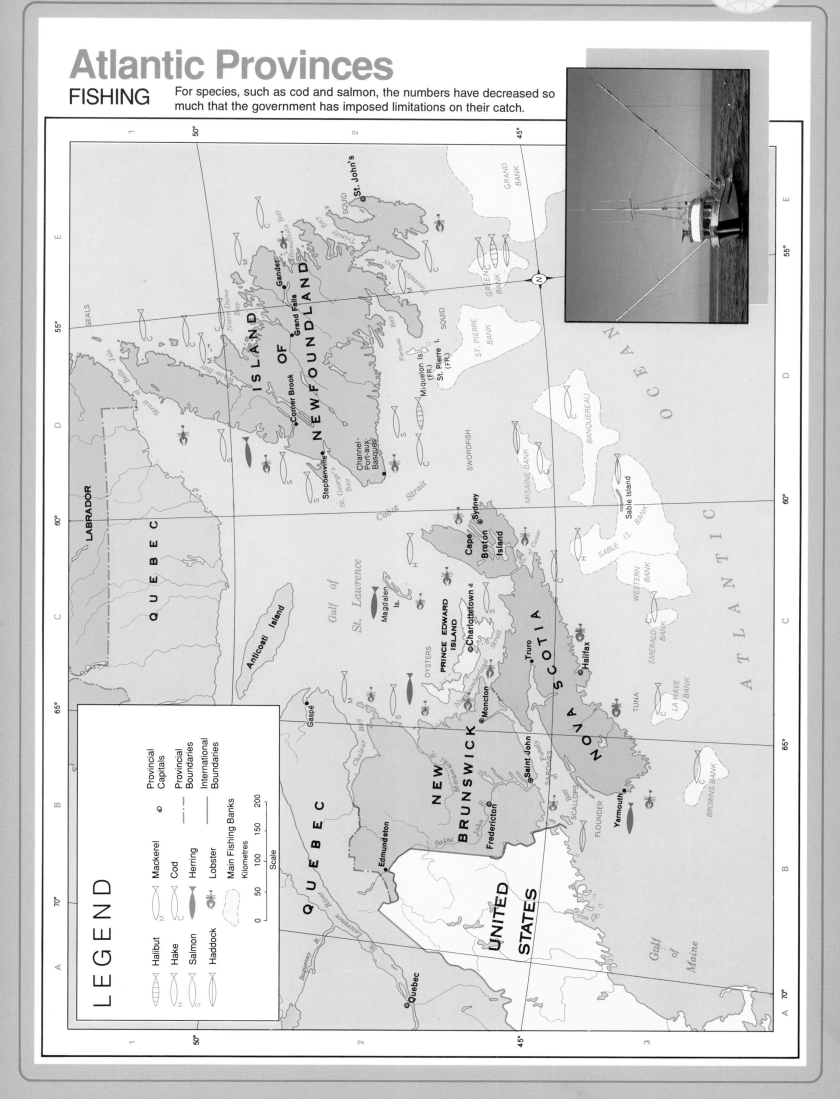

LEGEND

Halibut	Mackerel	●	Provincial Capitals
Hake	Cod	---·---	Provincial Boundaries
Salmon	Herring	— — —	International Boundaries
Haddock	Lobster		Main Fishing Banks

Kilometres

Scale

0   50   100   150   200

Map labels:

QUEBEC

LABRADOR

ISLAND OF NEWFOUNDLAND

Strait of Belle Isle
White Bay
Notre Dame Bay
Bonavista Bay
Trinity Bay
St. John's
Gander
Grand Falls
Corner Brook
Conception Bay
Placentia Bay
Fortune Bay
Channel-Port-aux-Basques
Stephenville
St. George's Bay
Cabot Strait

GRAND BANK
GREEN BANK
ST. PIERRE BANK
St. Pierre I. (FR.)
Miquelon Is. (FR.)

Anticosti Island
Gulf of St. Lawrence
Magdalen Is.
Gaspé
Chaleur Bay

PRINCE EDWARD ISLAND
Charlottetown
Sydney
Cape Breton Island
Strait of Canso
Northumberland Strait

NOVA SCOTIA
Truro
Halifax
Moncton
Sable Island
SABLE IS. BANK
MISAINE BANK
BANQUEREAU
WESTERN BANK
EMERALD BANK
LA HAVE BANK
BROWNS BANK

NEW BRUNSWICK
Saint John
Fredericton
Edmundston
Miramichi R.
Saint John R.

Yarmouth
Gulf of Maine

QUEBEC
Quebec
St. Lawrence River
Saguenay R.

UNITED STATES

ATLANTIC OCEAN

SEALS
SQUID
SWORDFISH
OYSTERS
TUNA
FLOUNDER
SCALLOPS
SARDINES

Quebec
TRANSPORTATION

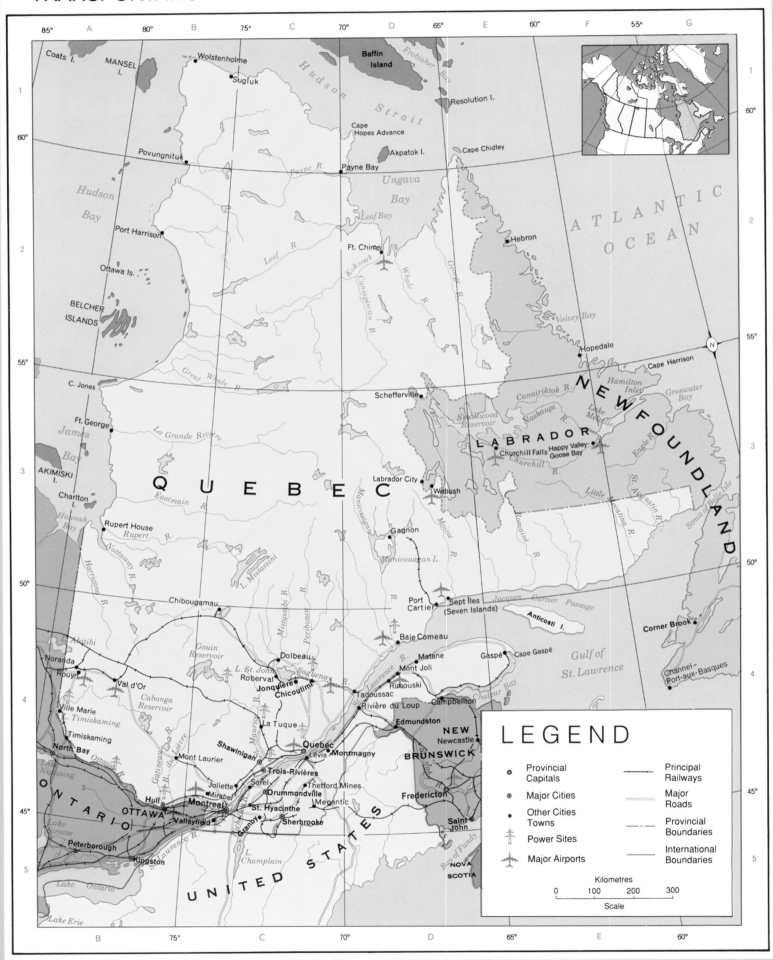

Quebec
LANDFORMS–Relief

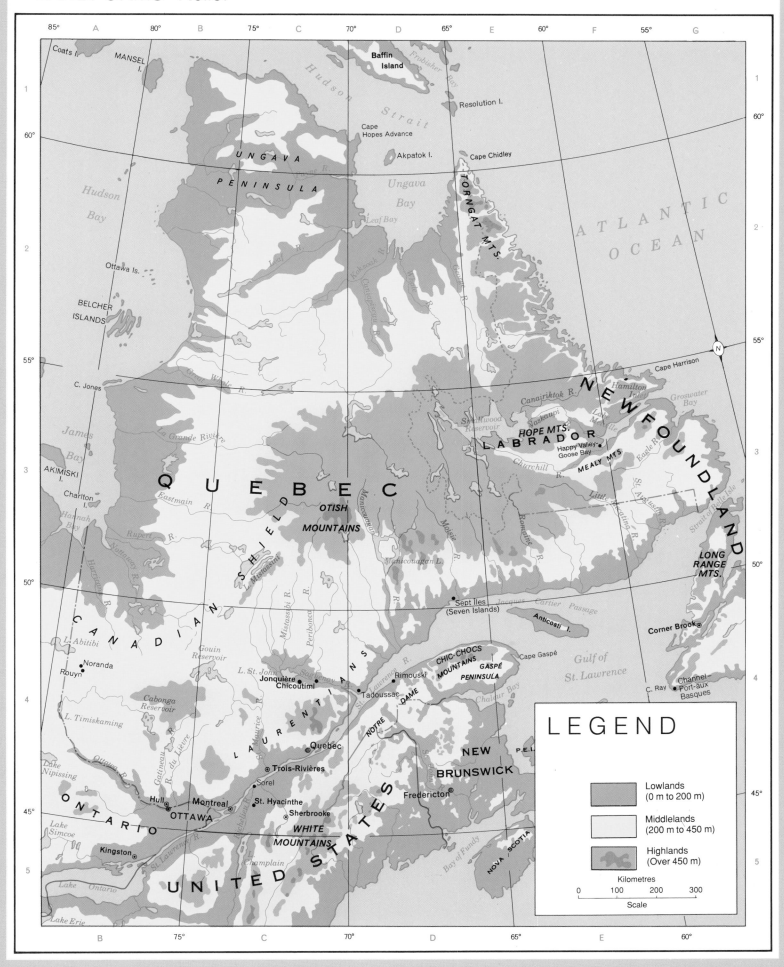

Coats I.
MANSEL I.
Baffin Island
Frobisher Bay
Hudson Strait
Resolution I.
Cape Hopes Advance
UNGAVA PENINSULA
Akpatok I.
Cape Chidley
Ungava Bay
TORNGAT MTS.
ATLANTIC OCEAN
Hudson Bay
Leaf Bay
Leaf R.
Ottawa Is.
BELCHER ISLANDS
N
C. Jones
Great Whale R.
Cape Harrison
Canairiktok R.
Hamilton Inlet
Groswater Bay
NEWFOUNDLAND
James Bay
La Grande Rivière
Smallwood Reservoir
Naskaupi R.
HOPE MTS.
LABRADOR
Happy Valley-Goose Bay
AKIMISKI I.
Eastmain R.
Churchill R.
MEALY MTS.
Charlton I.
QUEBEC
Eagle R.
Hannah Bay
Rupert R.
OTISH MOUNTAINS
Manicouagan R.
Little Mecatina R.
Strait of Belle Isle
Nottaway R.
CANADIAN SHIELD
L. Mistassini
Moisie R.
St. Augustin R.
Harricana R.
Manicouagan L.
Romaine R.
LONG RANGE MTS.
L. Abitibi
Mistassini R.
Sept Îles (Seven Islands)
Jacques Cartier Passage
Noranda
Gouin Reservoir
Peribonca R.
Anticosti I.
Corner Brook
Rouyn
Cabonga Reservoir
L. St. John
Saguenay R.
CHIC-CHOCS MOUNTAINS
Cape Gaspé
Gulf of St. Lawrence
C. Ray
Channel–Port-aux-Basques
L. Timiskaming
Jonquière
Chicoutimi
Rimouski
GASPÉ PENINSULA
Lake Nipissing
Gatineau R.
R. du Lièvre
Tadoussac
LAURENTIANS
DAME
St. Lawrence R.
Chaleur Bay
Ottawa R.
NOTRE
Quebec
NEW
P.E.I.
ONTARIO
Trois-Rivières
Sorel
BRUNSWICK
Hull
Montreal
St. Hyacinthe
NOVA SCOTIA
OTTAWA
Sherbrooke
Fredericton
Lake Simcoe
Richelieu R.
WHITE MOUNTAINS
Kingston
UNITED STATES
Bay of Fundy
Champlain
Lake Ontario
St. Lawrence R.
Lake Erie

LEGEND

Lowlands (0 m to 200 m)

Middlelands (200 m to 450 m)

Highlands (Over 450 m)

Kilometres
0   100   200   300
Scale

Quebec
MINING

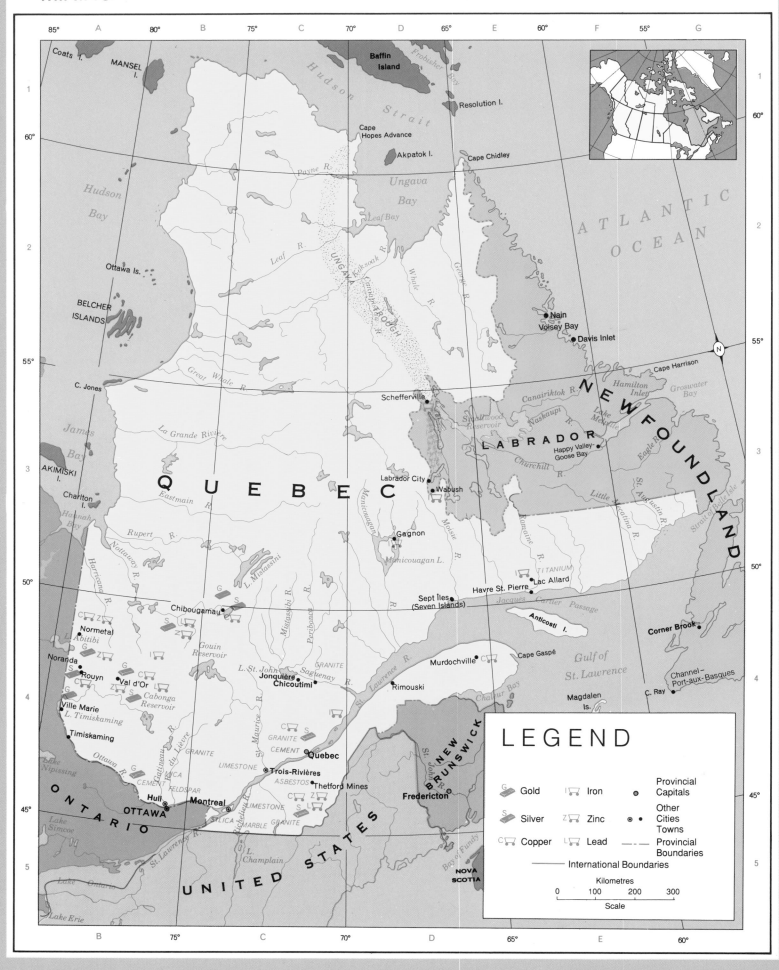

LEGEND

G Gold	Iron	•	Provincial Capitals
S Silver	Z Zinc	⊙	Other Cities
C Copper	Lead	•	Towns
		---	Provincial Boundaries
		—	International Boundaries

Kilometres
0   100   200   300
Scale

Quebec
FARMING and INDUSTRIES

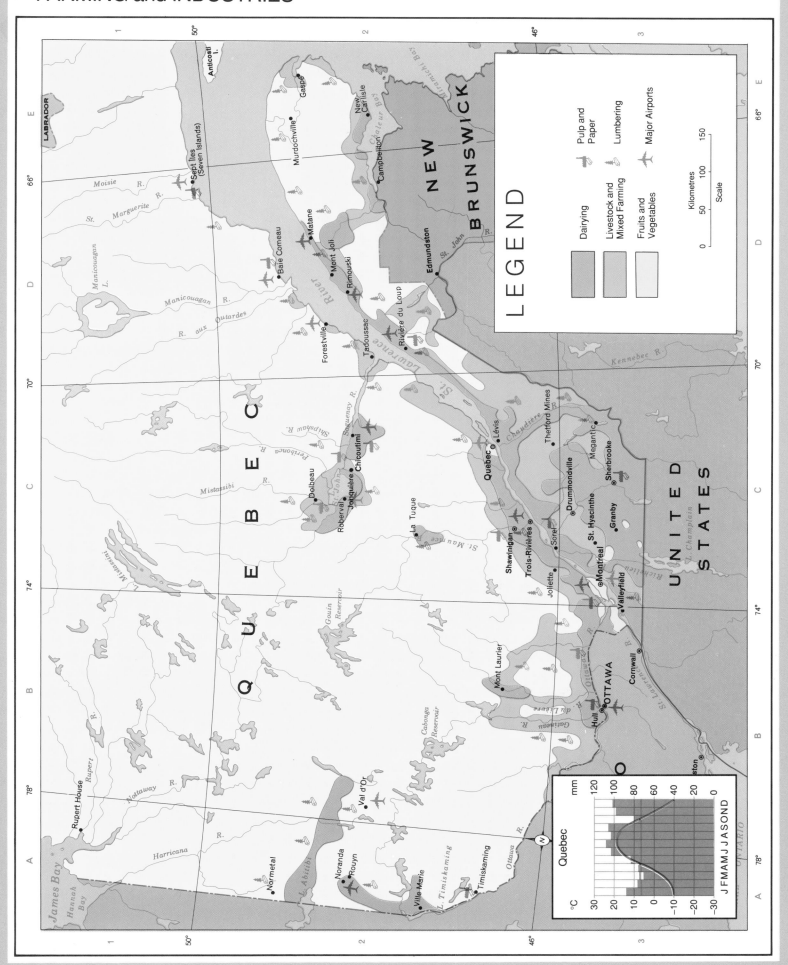

LABRADOR

Anticosti I.

Gaspé
New Carlisle
Murdochville
Campbellton
Chaleur Bay
Miramichi Bay

NEW BRUNSWICK

Matane
Mont Joli
Rimouski
Sept Îles (Seven Islands)
Baie Comeau
Edmundston
St. John R.
Moisie R.
St. Marguerite R.
Manicouagan L.
Manicouagan R.
R. aux Outardes

Forestville
Tadoussac
Rivière du Loup
Kennebec R.

Dolbeau
Chicoutimi
Jonquière
Roberval
Shipshaw R.
Saguenay R.
Péribonca R.
Mistassibi R.
St. John L.

Lévis
Thetford Mines
Mégantic
Sherbrooke
Chaudière R.
Québec
Drummondville
Granby
St. Hyacinthe

La Tuque
St. Maurice R.
Shawinigan
Trois-Rivières
Sorel
Joliette
Montréal
Valleyfield
Richelieu R.
L. Champlain

QUEBEC

UNITED STATES

L. Mistassini

Gouin Reservoir

Mont Laurier
du Lièvre R.
Cabonga Reservoir
Gatineau R.
Hull
OTTAWA
Cornwall
St. Lawrence R.
Ottawa R.

Rupert House
Rupert R.
Nottaway R.
Harricana R.
James Bay
Hannah Bay

Val d'Or
L. Abitibi
Normetal
Noranda
Rouyn
Ville-Marie
L. Timiskaming
Timiskaming
ONTARIO

LEGEND

Dairying	Pulp and Paper
Livestock and Mixed Farming	Lumbering
Fruits and Vegetables	Major Airports

Kilometres
0 50 100 150
Scale

Quebec

mm
120
100
80
60
40
20
0

°C
30
20
10
0
-10
-20
-30

J F M A M J J A S O N D

Southern Ontario
TRANSPORTATION

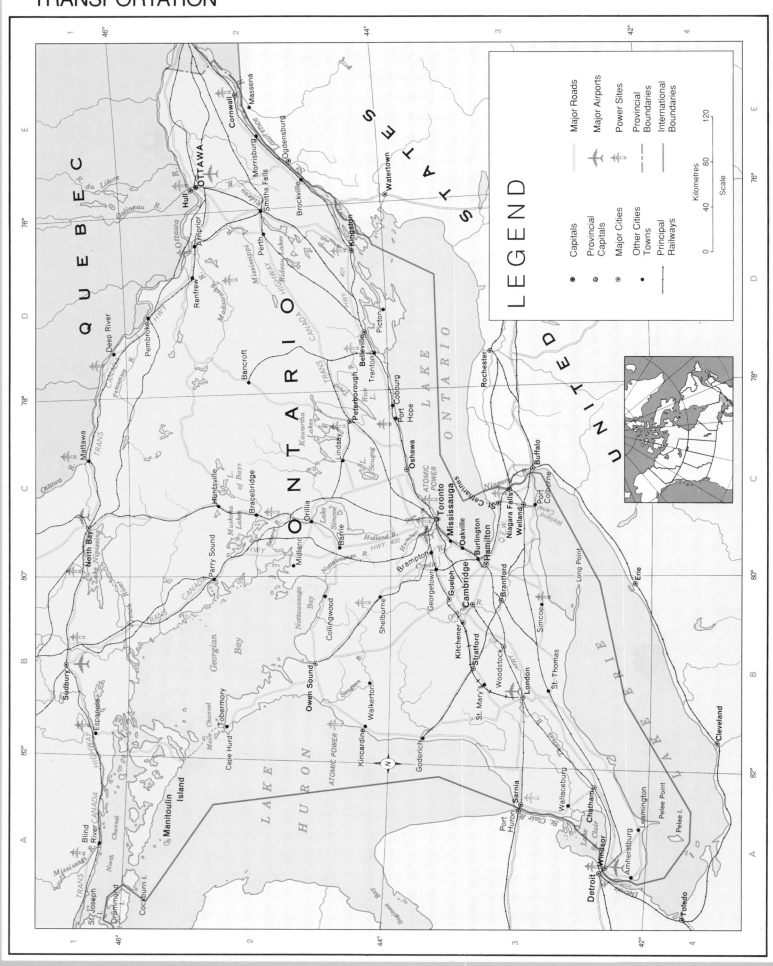

LEGEND

●	Capitals	—	Major Roads
●	Provincial Capitals	✈ ✈	Major Airports
◉	Major Cities		Power Sites
•	Other Cities Towns	---	Provincial Boundaries
—	Principal Railways		International Boundaries

Scale

Kilometres
0   40   80   120

Southern Ontario
LANDFORMS–Relief

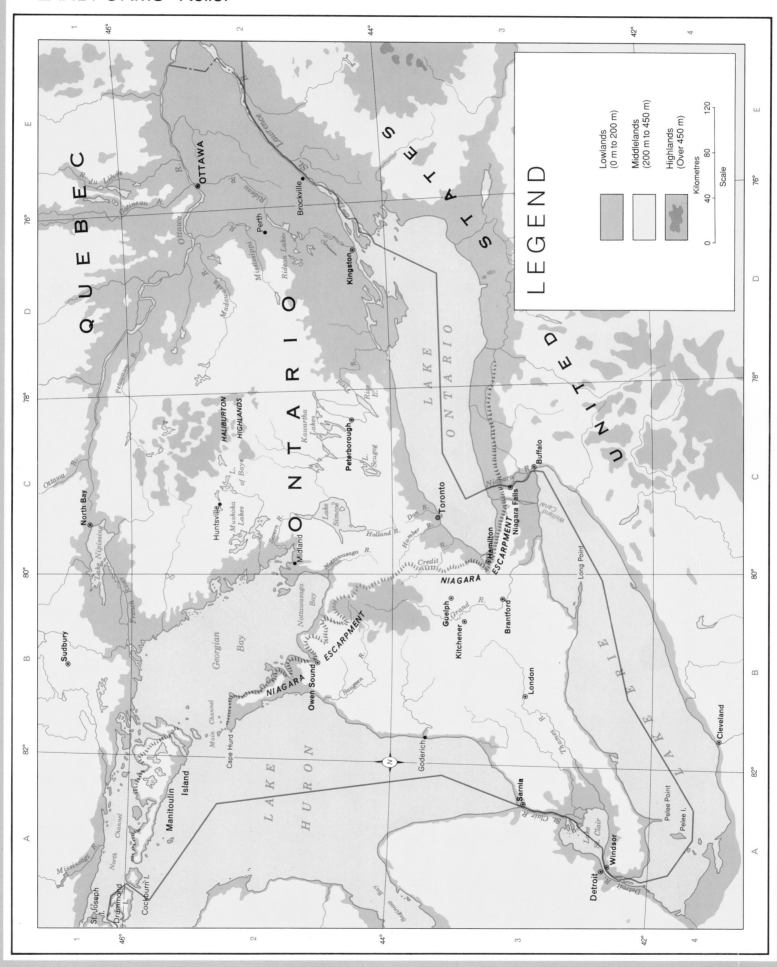

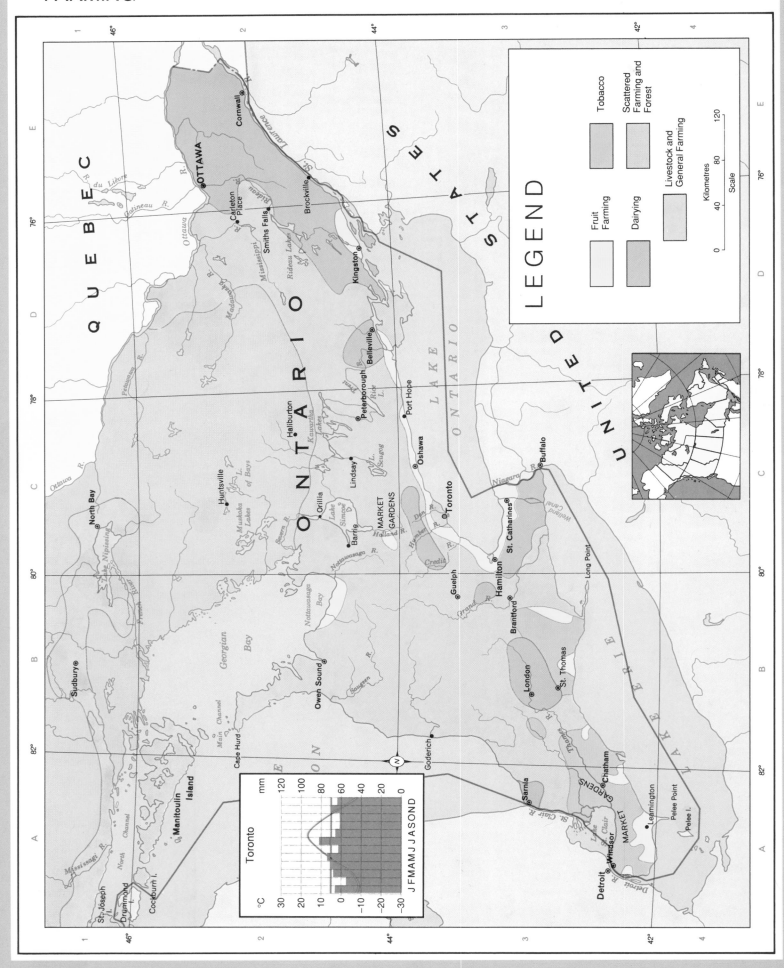

Southern Ontario
FARMING

LEGEND

Fruit Farming

Tobacco

Dairying

Scattered Farming and Forest

Livestock and General Farming

Scale

Kilometres
0 40 80 120

Toronto

Southern Ontario
MINING and INDUSTRIES

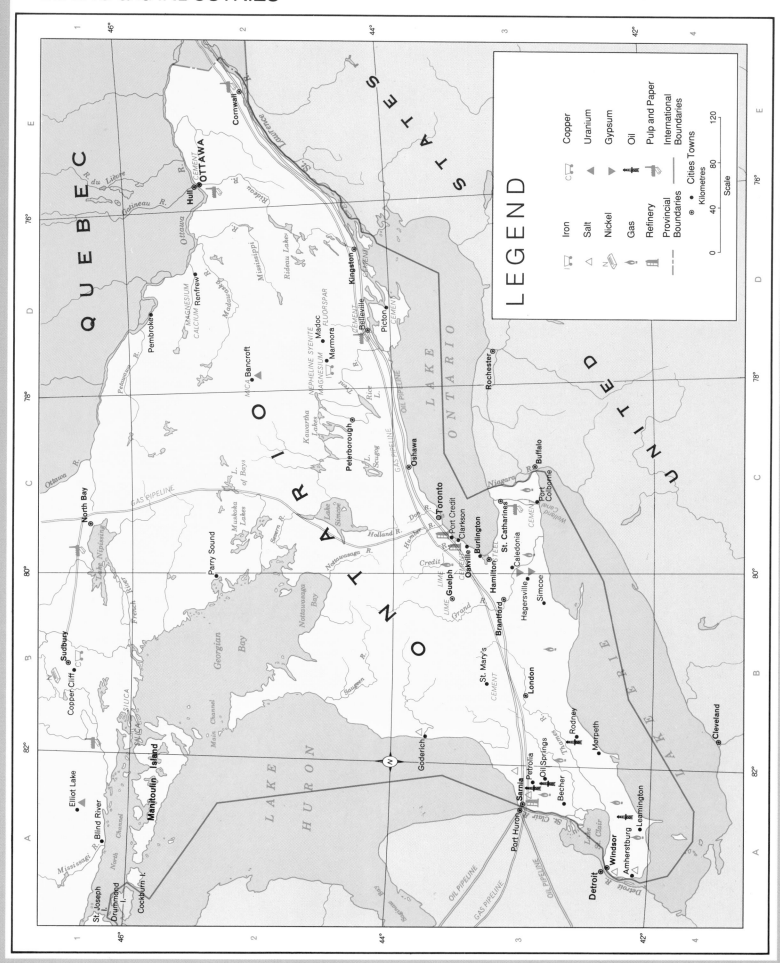

LEGEND

Iron	Copper	Pulp and Paper
Salt	Uranium	Oil
Nickel	Gypsum	International Boundaries
Gas	Refinery	Provincial Boundaries
		Cities Towns

Scale
Kilometres
0   40   80   120

Northern Ontario
TRANSPORTATION

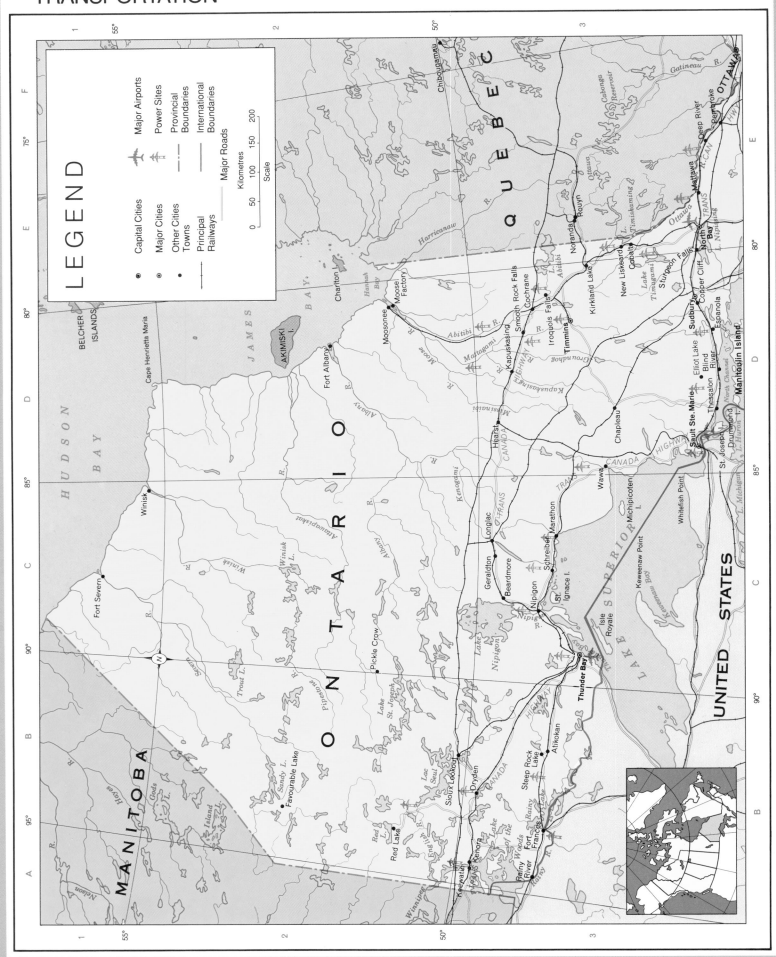

LEGEND

Capital Cities
Major Cities
Other Cities
Towns
Principal Railways

Major Airports
Power Sites
Provincial Boundaries
International Boundaries
Major Roads

Scale

Kilometres

0 50 100 150 200

QUEBEC

ONTARIO

MANITOBA

UNITED STATES

HUDSON BAY

JAMES BAY

LAKE SUPERIOR

BELCHER ISLANDS

AKIMISKI I.

Charlton I.

Cape Henrietta Maria

Hannah Bay

Moose Factory

Moosonee

Fort Albany

Winisk

Fort Severn

Pickle Crow

Favourable Lake
Sandy L.
Gods L.
Island L.

Red Lake
Red L.

Lac Seul

Sioux Lookout

Dryden

Kenora
Keewatin

Rainy River
Fort Frances

Atikokan
Steep Rock Lake

Thunder Bay

Nipigon
St. Ignace I.
Schreiber
Marathon
Beardmore
Geraldton
Longlac

Hearst
Kapuskasing
Smooth Rock Falls
Cochrane
Iroquois Falls
Timmins

Chapleau

Wawa

Michipicoten I.
Whitefish Point
Keweenaw Point
Keweenaw Bay
Isle Royale

Sault Ste. Marie
St. Joseph I.
Drummond I.
Manitoulin Island
Espanola
Blind River
Thessalon
Elliot Lake
Copper Cliff
Sudbury

North Bay
Sturgeon Falls
New Liskeard
Cobalt
Kirkland Lake
Noranda
Rouyn

Chibougamau

Mattawa
Deep River
Pentroke
OTTAWA

Gatineau R.
Cabonga Reservoir
Ottawa R.
L. Timiskaming
L. Nipissing
L. Abitibi
Abitibi R.
Harricanaw R.
Moose R.
Mattagami R.
Groundhog R.
Kapuskasing R.
Mississippi R.
Kenogami R.
Albany R.
Attawapiskat R.
Winisk L.
Winisk R.
Severn R.
Pipestone R.
Trout L.
St. Joseph Lake
Lake of the Woods
Rainy Lake
L. Nipigon
Nipigon R.
Lake Nipigon

Nelson R.
Hayes R.

L. Michigan
L. Huron
North Channel
Georgian Bay

TRANS CANADA HIGHWAY

Northern Ontario
LANDFORMS–Relief

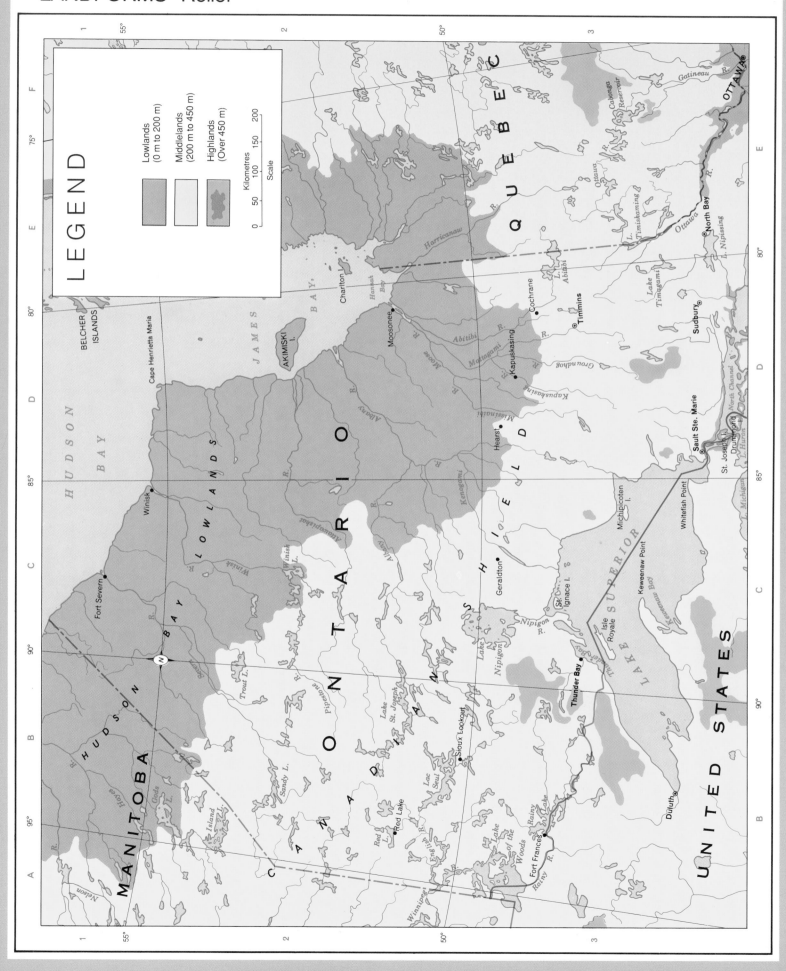

Northern Ontario
MINING and INDUSTRIES

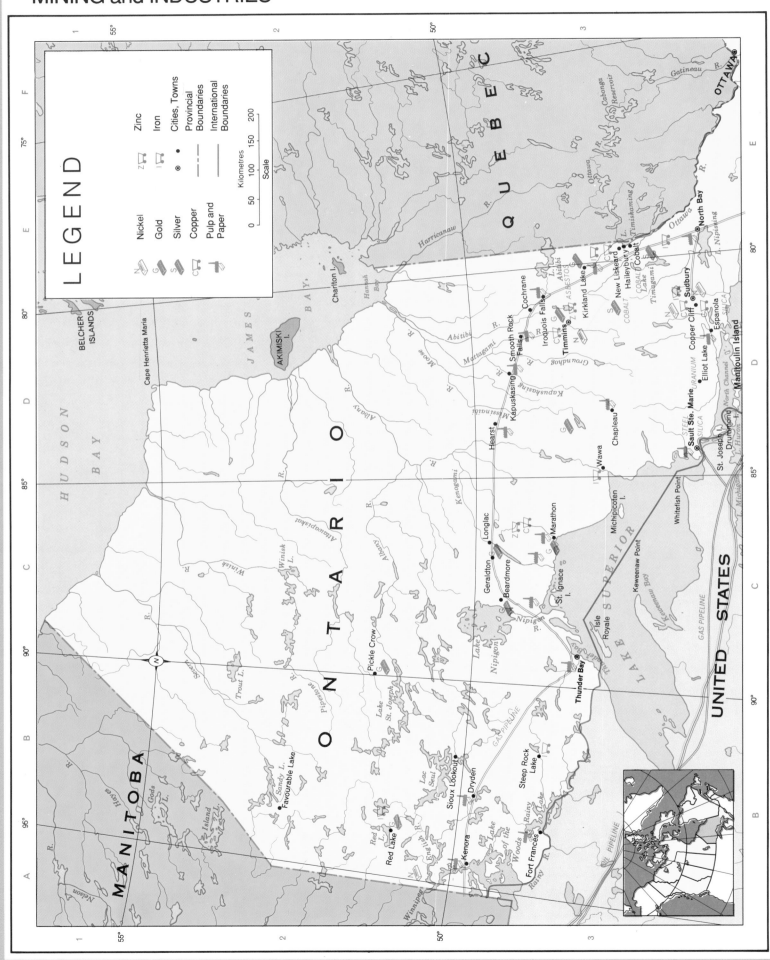

LEGEND

N Nickel	Z Zinc
G Gold	I Iron
S Silver	• Cities, Towns
C Copper	◉
Pulp and Paper	Provincial Boundaries
	International Boundaries

Scale
Kilometres
0 50 100 150 200

QUEBEC

ONTARIO

MANITOBA

UNITED STATES

HUDSON BAY

JAMES BAY

LAKE SUPERIOR

BELCHER ISLANDS

AKIMISKI I.

Charlton I.

Cape Henrietta Maria

Ottawa

North Bay

New Liskeard
Haileybury
Cobalt
COBALT
Kirkland Lake
Cochrane
Iroquois Falls
Smooth Rock Falls
Timmins
Kapuskasing
Hearst
Chapleau
Wawa
Sudbury
Copper Cliff
Espanola
Elliot Lake
Sault Ste. Marie
St. Joseph I.
Manitoulin Island
Drummond I.

Longlac
Marathon
Geraldton
Beardmore
St. Ignace I.
Nipigon
Michipicoten I.
Whitefish Point
Keweenaw Point
Keweenaw Bay
Isle Royale

Thunder Bay
Steep Rock Lake
Pickle Crow
Sioux Lookout
Dryden
Red Lake
Kenora
Fort Frances

GAS PIPELINE

Manitoba
TRANSPORTATION

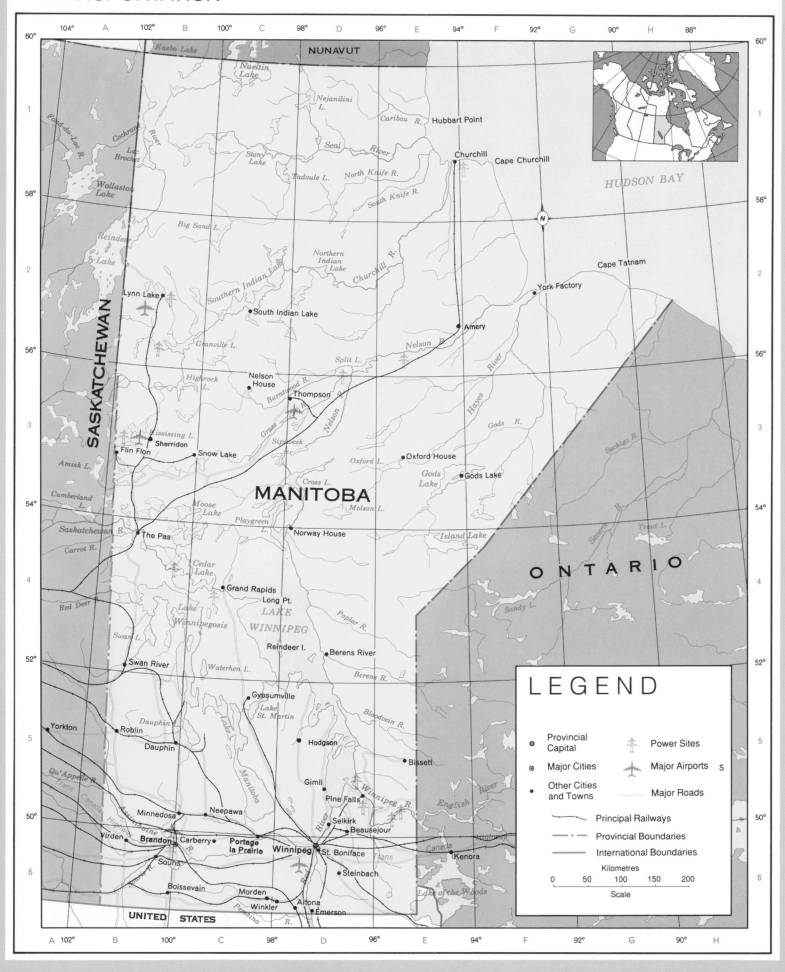

NUNAVUT

Kasba Lake

Nueltin Lake

Fond-du-Lac R.

Cochrane River

Nejanilini L.

Caribou R. Hubbart Point

Lac Brochet

Stony Lake

Seal River

Churchill Cape Churchill

Wollaston Lake

Tadoule L. *North Knife R.*

South Knife R.

HUDSON BAY

Reindeer Lake

Big Sand L.

N

SASKATCHEWAN

Northern Indian Lake

Cape Tatnam

Lynn Lake

Southern Indian Lake

Churchill R.

York Factory

South Indian Lake

Nelson R.

Amery

Granville L.

Split L.

Hayes River

Highrock L.

Nelson House

Gods R.

Flin Flon *Fississing L.* Sherridon

Burntwood R. Thompson

Sachigo R.

Snow Lake

Grass *Sipiwesk*

Nelson R.

Oxford L. Oxford House

Gods Lake

Amisk L.

Cross L.

Gods Lake

Cumberland L.

MANITOBA

Molson L.

Saskatchewan R.

Moose Lake

Playgreen L.

Norway House

Island Lake

Severn R.

Trout L.

Carrot R.

The Pas

ONTARIO

Red Deer

Cedar Lake

Grand Rapids
Long Pt.

Sandy L.

Lake Winnipegosis

LAKE WINNIPEG

Poplar R.

Swan L.

Reindeer I.

Berens River

Swan River

Waterhen L.

Berens R.

Gypsumville

Lake St. Martin

Bloodvein R.

Yorkton *Dauphin L.*

Roblin

Hodgson

English River

Dauphin

Bissett

Qu'Appelle R.

Gimli

Winnipeg R.

Pine Falls

Trans

Minnedosa Neepawa

Selkirk

Manitoba

Virden Brandon Carberry

Portage
la Prairie Winnipeg St. Boniface

Beausejour

Souris

Canada Kenora

Trans *Red River*

Boissevain

Steinbach

Lake of the Woods

Morden

Altona

Winkler Emerson

Pembina R.

UNITED STATES

LEGEND

- ● Provincial Capital
- ◉ Major Cities
- • Other Cities and Towns
- ⟰ Power Sites
- ✈ Major Airports S
- Major Roads
- Principal Railways
- Provincial Boundaries
- International Boundaries

Kilometres

0   50   100   150   200

Scale

Manitoba
LANDFORMS–Relief

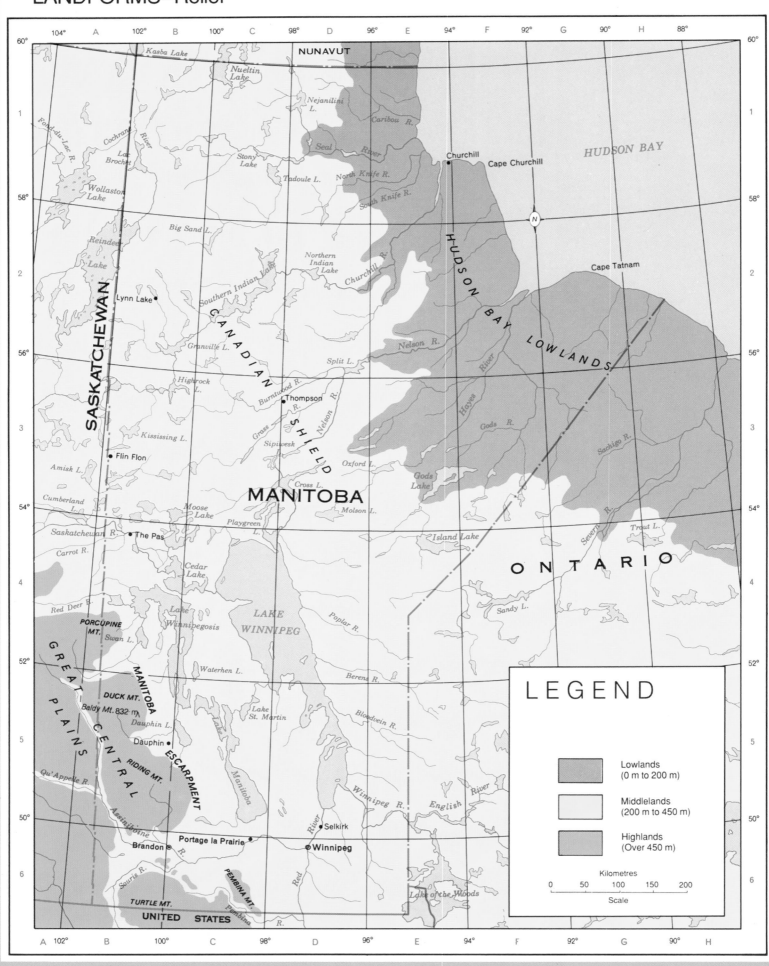

NUNAVUT

Kasba Lake

Nueltin Lake

Nejanilini L.

Caribou R.

Fond-du-Lac R.

Cochrane River

Lac Brochet

Stony Lake

Seal River

North Knife R.

Churchill

Cape Churchill

HUDSON BAY

Wollaston Lake

Tadoule L.

South Knife R.

Big Sand L.

Reindeer Lake

Northern Indian Lake

Churchill R.

HUDSON BAY LOWLANDS

Cape Tatnam

SASKATCHEWAN

Lynn Lake

Southern Indian Lake

CANADIAN

Nelson R.

Hayes River

Granville L.

Highrock L.

Burntwood R.

Thompson

Gross R.

Nelson R.

SHIELD

Gods R.

Sachigo R.

Kississing L.

Sipiwesk L.

Flin Flon

Oxford L.

Gods Lake

Amisk L.

Cross L.

MANITOBA

Molson L.

Cumberland L.

Moose Lake

Playgreen L.

Split L.

Island Lake

Severn R.

Trout L.

Saskatchewan R.

The Pas

ONTARIO

Carrot R.

Cedar Lake

Red Deer R.

Lake Winnipegosis

LAKE WINNIPEG

Poplar R.

Sandy L.

PORCUPINE MT.

Swan L.

GREAT

DUCK MT.

Baldy Mt. 832 m

Dauphin L.

Waterhen L.

Berens R.

Lake St. Martin

Bloodvein R.

PLAINS

Dauphin

CENTRAL

RIDING MT.

Qu'Appelle R.

ESCARPMENT

Lake Manitoba

Winnipeg R.

English River

Assiniboine R.

River

Selkirk

Portage la Prairie

Winnipeg

Brandon

R.

Souris R.

PEMBINA MT.

Red River

Lake of the Woods

TURTLE MT.

Pembina R.

UNITED STATES

LEGEND

	Lowlands (0 m to 200 m)
	Middlelands (200 m to 450 m)
	Highlands (Over 450 m)

Kilometres

0   50   100   150   200

Scale

Manitoba
FARMING

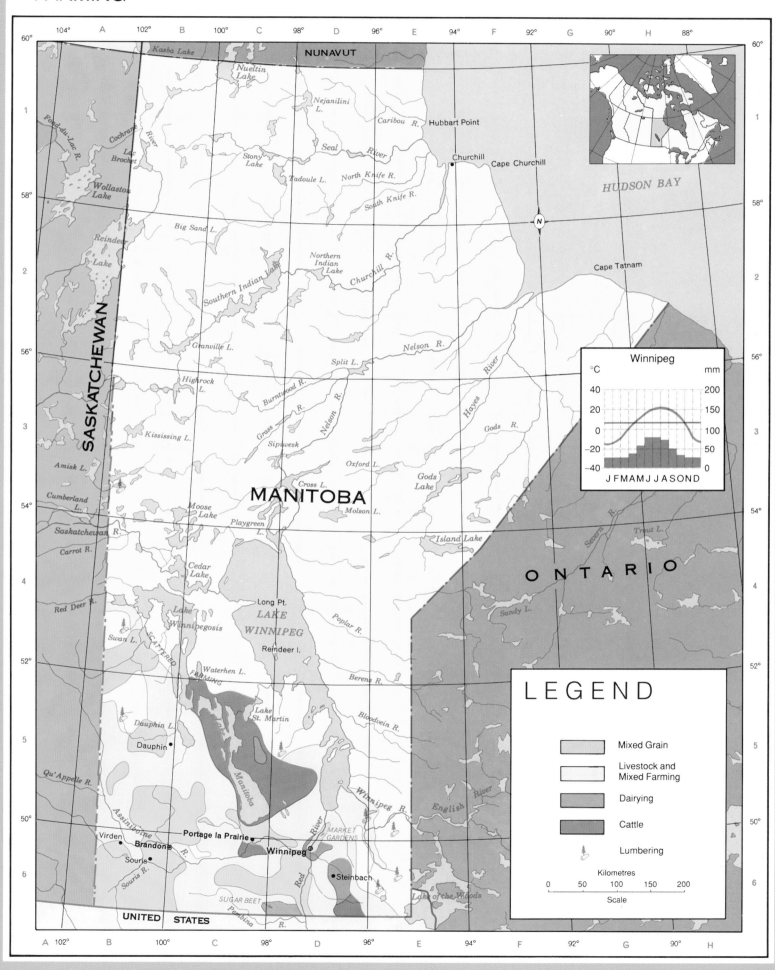

NUNAVUT

Kasba Lake
Nueltin Lake
Nejanilini L.
Caribou R.
Hubbart Point
Fond-du-Lac R.
Cochrane River
Lac Brochet
Stony Lake
Seal River
Churchill
Cape Churchill
Wollaston Lake
Tadoule L.
North Knife R.
South Knife R.

HUDSON BAY

N

Big Sand L.

Reindeer Lake

Northern Indian Lake
Churchill R.
Cape Tatnam

SASKATCHEWAN

Southern Indian Lake

Nelson R.
Granville L.
Split L.
Nelson R.
Highrock L.
Burntwood R.
Hayes River
Amisk L.
Kississing L.
Grass R.
Gods R.
Sipiwesk
Cumberland L.
Oxford L.
Gods Lake
Saskatchewan R.
Cross L.
MANITOBA
Molson L.
Carrot R.
Moose Lake
Playgreen L.
Island Lake
Severn R.
Trout L.

ONTARIO

Cedar Lake
Sandy L.
Red Deer R.
Lake Winnipegosis
LAKE WINNIPEG
Poplar R.
Swan L.
SCATTERED
Reindeer I.
FARMING
Waterhen L.
Berens R.
Dauphin L.
Lake St. Martin
Bloodvein R.
Dauphin
Lake Manitoba
Qu'Appelle R.
Winnipeg R.
English River
Assiniboine R.
Virden
Portage la Prairie
MARKET GARDENS
Brandon
Winnipeg
Souris
Red River
Souris R.
Steinbach
SUGAR BEET
Lake of the Woods
Pembina R.

UNITED STATES

Winnipeg

°C / mm
J F M A M J J A S O N D

LEGEND

Mixed Grain

Livestock and Mixed Farming

Dairying

Cattle

Lumbering

Kilometres
0   50   100   150   200
Scale

Manitoba
MINING and INDUSTRIES

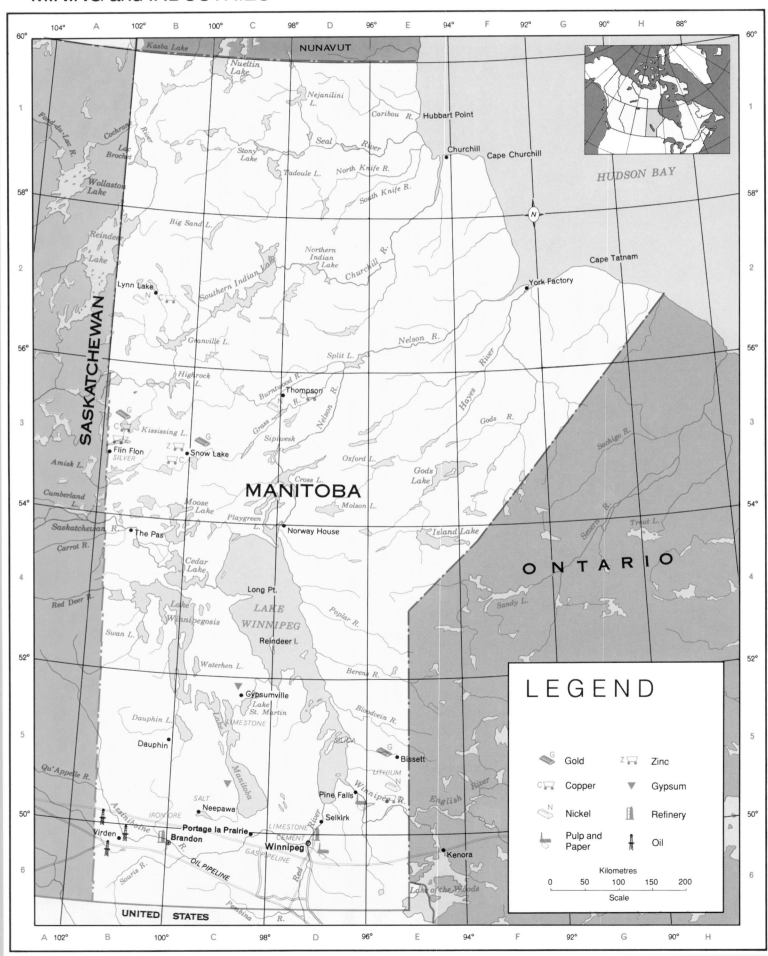

NUNAVUT

Kasba Lake

Nueltin Lake

Nejanilini L.

Caribou R. — Hubbart Point

Cochrane Seal River

Fond-du-Lac R.

Lac Brochet

Stony Lake

Tadoule L.

North Knife R.

Churchill — Cape Churchill

Wollaston Lake

South Knife R.

HUDSON BAY

Reindeer Lake

Big Sand L.

Northern Indian Lake

Churchill R.

N

Lynn Lake

Southern Indian Lake

Nelson R.

Cape Tatnam

York Factory

SASKATCHEWAN

Granville L.

Split L.

Highrock L.

Burntwood R. — Thompson

Hayes River

Gods R.

Kississing L.

Grass R.

Sipiwesk

Nelson R.

Flin Flon
SILVER

Snow Lake

Oxford L.

Gods Lake

Sechigo R.

Amisk L.

Cross L.

MANITOBA

Molson L.

Cumberland L.

Moose Lake

Saskatchewan R.

The Pas

Playgreen L. — Norway House

Island Lake

Trout L.

Carrot R.

Cedar Lake

ONTARIO

Red Deer R.

Lake Winnipegosis

Long Pt.

LAKE WINNIPEG

Poplar R.

Sandy L.

Swan L.

Reindeer I.

Waterhen L.

Berens R.

Severn R.

English River

Gypsumville
Lake St. Martin

Bloodvein R.

LIMESTONE

Dauphin L.

SILICA

Bissett

Dauphin

LITHIUM
N

Qu'Appelle R.

Manitoba

Pine Falls

Winnipeg R.

SALT

Neepawa

Selkirk

Kenora

Virden

IRON ORE

Portage la Prairie

LIMESTONE

Brandon

Assiniboine R.

CEMENT

Winnipeg

Red River

Souris R.

OIL PIPELINE

GAS PIPELINE

Pembina R.

Lake of the Woods

UNITED STATES

LEGEND

G Gold		Z Zinc	
C Copper		Gypsum	
N Nickel		Refinery	
Pulp and Paper		Oil	

Kilometres

0 50 100 150 200

Scale

Saskatchewan
TRANSPORTATION

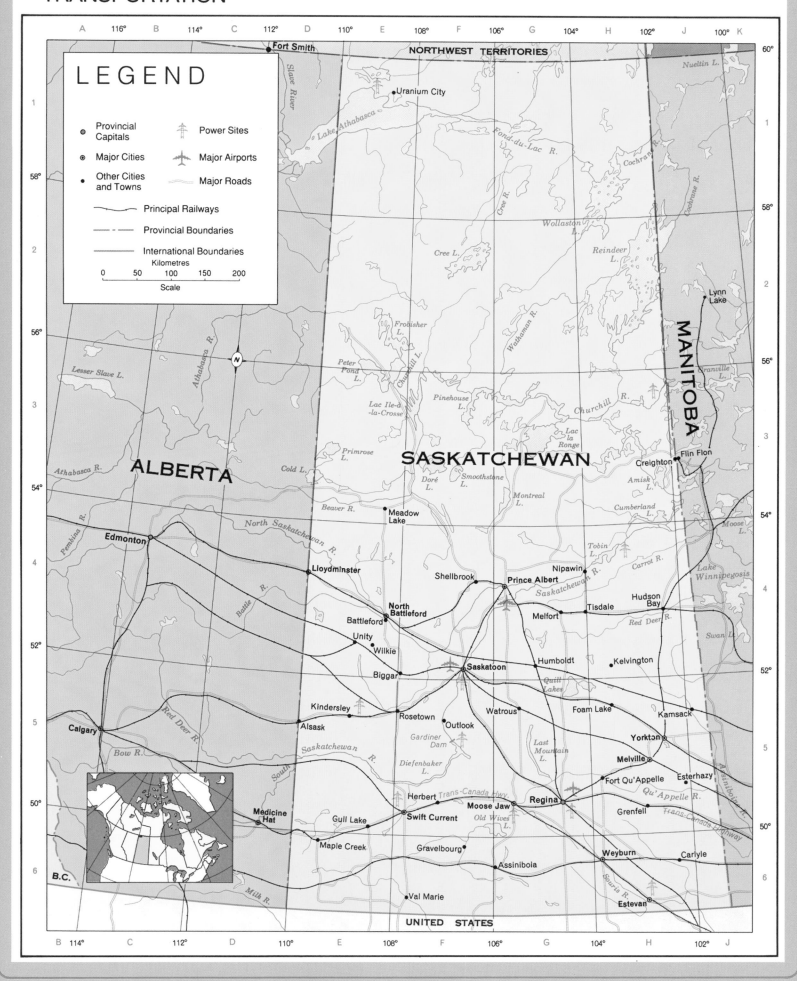

LEGEND

- ● Provincial Capitals
- ◉ Major Cities
- • Other Cities and Towns
- Power Sites
- Major Airports
- Major Roads
- ⌇⌇⌇ Principal Railways
- —·—·— Provincial Boundaries
- ——— International Boundaries

Kilometres
0 50 100 150 200
Scale

NORTHWEST TERRITORIES

Fort Smith

Uranium City

Lake Athabasca

Slave River

Fond-du-Lac R.

Cree R.

Nueltin L.

Cochrane R.

Cree L.

Wollaston L.

Reindeer L.

Cochrane R.

Wathaman R.

Frobisher L.

Peter Pond L.

Churchill L.

Lac Ile-à-la-Crosse

Pinehouse L.

Lac la Ronge

Churchill R.

Granville L.

Lynn Lake

MANITOBA

Primrose L.

Cold L.

SASKATCHEWAN

Doré L.

Smoothstone L.

Montreal L.

Amisk L.

Cumberland L.

Moose L.

Flin Flon

Creighton

ALBERTA

Athabasca R.

Lesser Slave L.

Athabasca R.

Pembina R.

Beaver R.

North Saskatchewan R.

Meadow Lake

Tobin L.

Carrot R.

Lake Winnipegosis

Edmonton

Lloydminster

Battle R.

Shellbrook

Prince Albert

Nipawin

Saskatchewan R.

Hudson Bay

Swan L.

North Battleford
Battleford

Melfort

Tisdale

Red Deer R.

Unity

Wilkie

Humboldt

Kelvington

Biggar

Saskatoon

Quill Lakes

Foam Lake

Kamsack

Calgary

Red Deer R.

Kindersley

Rosetown

Watrous

Last Mountain L.

Yorkton

Alsask

Outlook

Bow R.

Saskatchewan R.

Gardiner Dam

Diefenbaker L.

Melville

Esterhazy

Fort Qu'Appelle

Qu'Appelle R.

Assiniboine R.

Herbert

Trans-Canada Hwy.

Moose Jaw

Regina

Grenfell

Trans-Canada Highway

Medicine Hat

Gull Lake

Swift Current

Old Wives L.

Maple Creek

Gravelbourg

Weyburn

Carlyle

B.C.

Milk R.

Val Marie

Assiniboia

Souris R.

Estevan

UNITED STATES

Saskatchewan
LANDFORMS–Relief

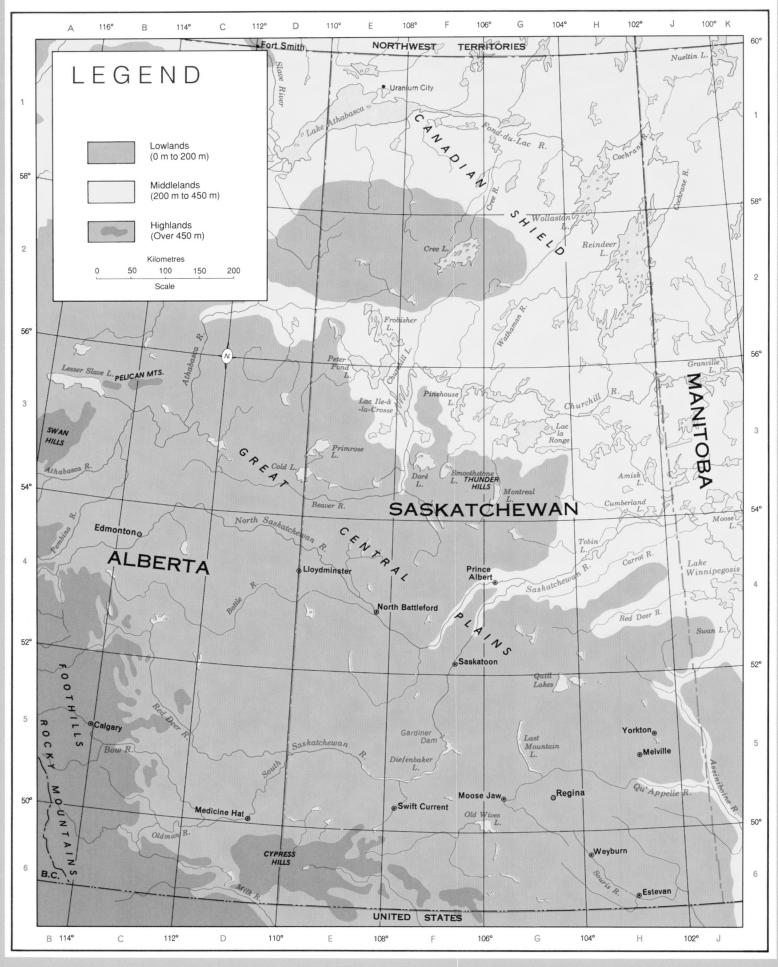

LEGEND

Lowlands
(0 m to 200 m)

Middlelands
(200 m to 450 m)

Highlands
(Over 450 m)

Kilometres

0   50   100   150   200

Scale

NORTHWEST   TERRITORIES

Fort Smith

Slave River

Uranium City

Lake Athabasca

CANADIAN   SHIELD

Nueltin L.

Fond-du-Lac R.

Cochrane R.

Cree R.

Wollaston L.

Cree L.

Reindeer L.

Cochrane R.

Wathaman R.

Frobisher L.

Granville L.

Peter Pond L.

Pinehouse L.

MANITOBA

Lesser Slave L.

PELICAN MTS.

Athabasca R.

N

Lac Ile-à-la-Crosse

Churchill L.

Churchill R.

SWAN HILLS

Primrose L.

Lac la Ronge

Amisk L.

Athabasca R.

GREAT

Cold L.

Doré L.

Smoothstone L.
THUNDER HILLS

Cumberland L.

Moose L.

Pembina R.

Beaver R.

Montreal L.

SASKATCHEWAN

Edmonton

North Saskatchewan R.

CENTRAL

Tobin L.

Saskatchewan R.

ALBERTA

Lloydminster

Battle R.

Prince Albert

Carrot R.

Lake Winnipegosis

Red Deer R.

North Battleford

PLAINS

Swan L.

Saskatoon

Quill Lakes

Red Deer R.

Calgary

FOOTHILLS

Bow R.

South Saskatchewan R.

Gardiner Dam

Last Mountain L.

Yorkton

Melville

ROCKY

Diefenbaker L.

Regina

Assiniboine R.

Medicine Hat

Moose Jaw

Qu'Appelle R.

MOUNTAINS

Oldman R.

Swift Current

Old Wives L.

Weyburn

B.C.

CYPRESS HILLS

Milk R.

Souris R.

Estevan

UNITED   STATES

Saskatchewan
FARMING

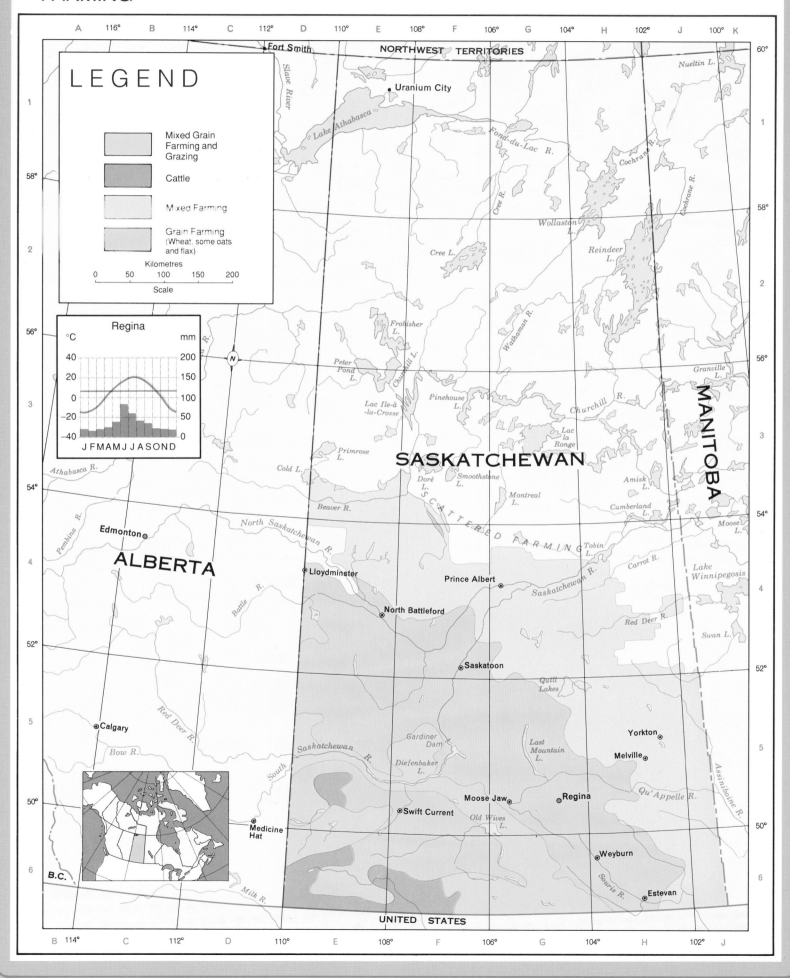

LEGEND

Mixed Grain Farming and Grazing

Cattle

Mixed Farming

Grain Farming (Wheat, some oats and flax)

Kilometres

0 50 100 150 200

Scale

Regina

°C / mm

40 / 200
20 / 150
0 / 100
-20 / 50
-40 / 0

J F M A M J J A S O N D

NORTHWEST TERRITORIES

Fort Smith
Uranium City
Nueltin L.
Slave River
Lake Athabasca
Fond-du-Lac R.
Cochrane R.
Cree R.
Wollaston L.
Cree L.
Reindeer L.
Wathaman R.
Frobisher L.
Peter Pond L.
Churchill L.
Granville L.
Pinehouse L.
Lac Ile-à-la-Crosse
Churchill R.
MANITOBA
SASKATCHEWAN
Lac la Ronge
Amisk L.
Primrose L.
Doré L.
Smoothstone L.
Montreal L.
Cumberland L.
Cold L.
Beaver R.
Moose L.
SCATTERED FARMING
North Saskatchewan R.
Tobin L.
Saskatchewan R.
Carrot R.
Lake Winnipegosis
Athabasca R.
ALBERTA
Edmonton
Lloydminster
Prince Albert
North Battleford
Red Deer R.
Swan L.
Pembina R.
Battle R.
Saskatoon
Quill Lakes
Red Deer R.
Calgary
Gardiner Dam
Last Mountain L.
Yorkton
Bow R.
Diefenbaker L.
Melville
South Saskatchewan R.
Moose Jaw
Regina
Qu'Appelle R.
Swift Current
Old Wives L.
Assiniboine R.
Medicine Hat
Weyburn
B.C.
Souris R.
Estevan
Milk R.

UNITED STATES

Saskatchewan
MINING and INDUSTRIES

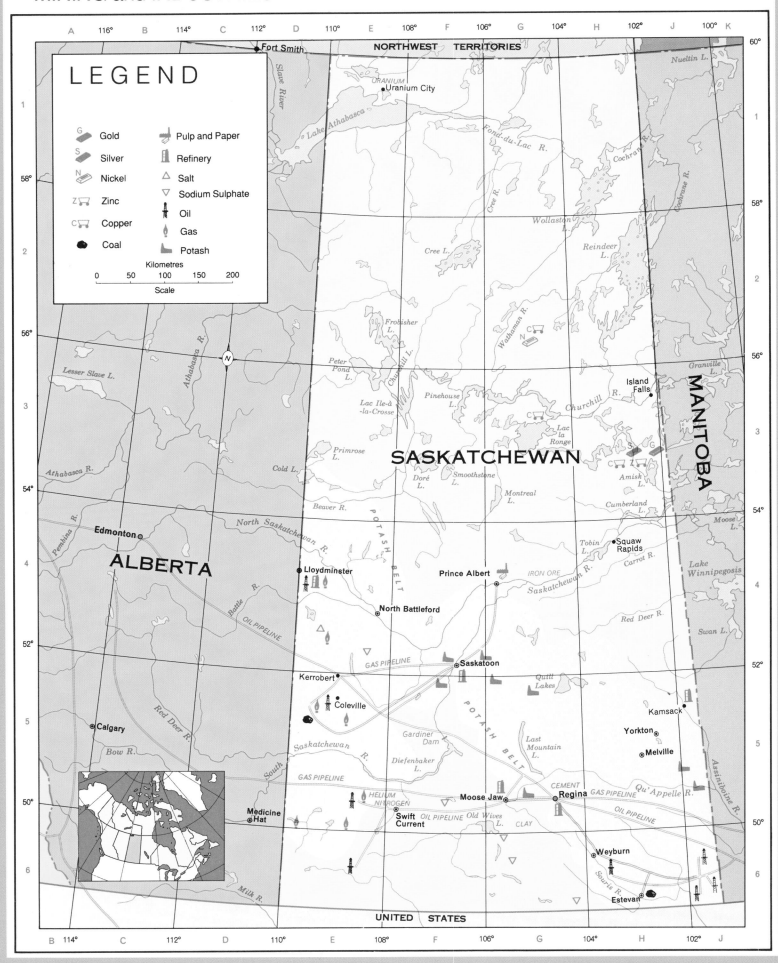

LEGEND

G Gold	Pulp and Paper
S Silver	Refinery
N Nickel	△ Salt
Z Zinc	▽ Sodium Sulphate
C Copper	Oil
Coal	Gas
	Potash

Kilometres
0   50   100   150   200
Scale

NORTHWEST TERRITORIES

Fort Smith

Nueltin L.

URANIUM
Uranium City

Lake Athabasca

Slave River

Fond-du-Lac R.

Cochrane R.

Cree R.

Wollaston

Reindeer L.

Cree L.

Frobisher L.

Peter Pond L.

Churchill L.

Pinehouse L.

Lac Ile-à-la-Crosse

N C
Wathaman R.

Granville L.

Island Falls

Churchill R.

Lac la Ronge

C
Amisk L.

S G
C Z

SASKATCHEWAN

MANITOBA

Lesser Slave L.

Athabasca R.

Primrose L.

Cold L.

Doré L.

Smoothstone L.

Montreal L.

Cumberland L.

Moose L.

Athabasca R.

Beaver R.

North Saskatchewan R.

POTASH BELT

Edmonton

ALBERTA

Lloydminster

Prince Albert

IRON ORE
Saskatchewan R.

Squaw Rapids

Tobin L.

Carrot R.

Lake Winnipegosis

North Battleford

Red Deer R.

Swan L.

Pembina R.

Battle R.

OIL PIPELINE

△

▽

GAS PIPELINE

Saskatoon

Quill Lakes

Kamsack

Kerrobert

Coleville

Calgary

Red Deer R.

Bow R.

Gardiner Dam

Diefenbaker L.

Saskatchewan R.

POTASH BELT

Last Mountain L.

Yorkton

Melville

South Saskatchewan R.

GAS PIPELINE

HELIUM NITROGEN

Moose Jaw

Old Wives L.

CEMENT GAS PIPELINE

Regina

Qu'Appelle R.

Assiniboine R.

Medicine Hat

Swift Current

OIL PIPELINE

CLAY

OIL PIPELINE

▽

Weyburn

▽

Souris R.

Milk R.

Estevan

UNITED STATES

Alberta
TRANSPORTATION

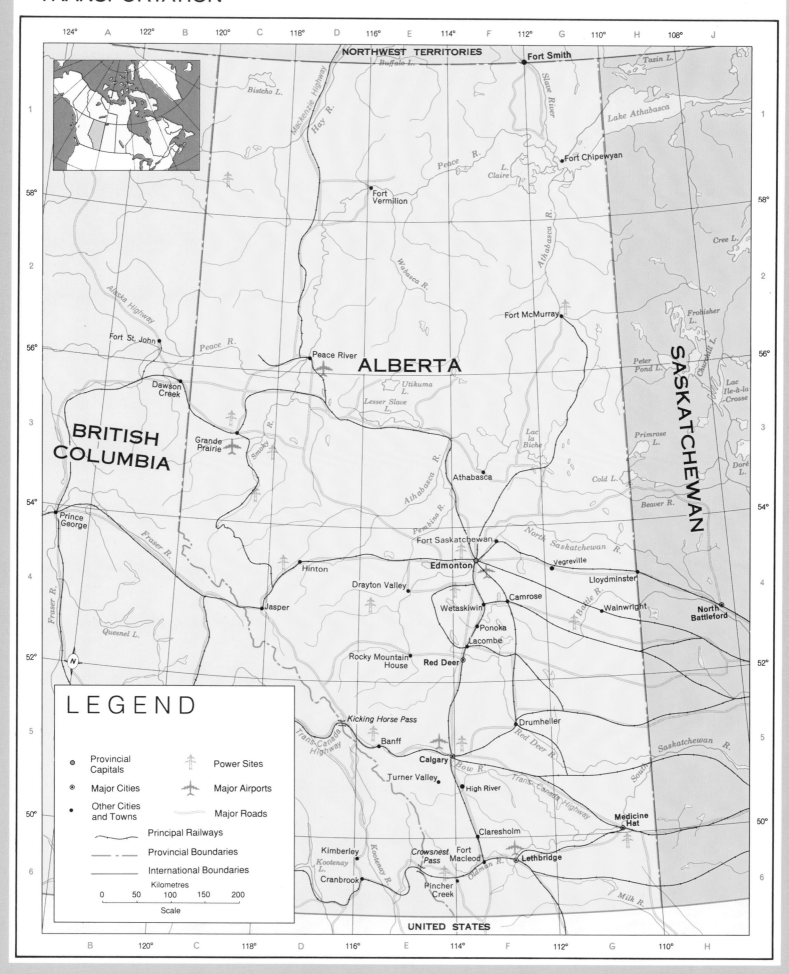

NORTHWEST TERRITORIES

Fort Smith

Buffalo L.

Bistcho L.

Tazin L.

Lake Athabasca

Fort Chipewyan

L. Claire

Cree L.

Fort Vermilion

Fort McMurray

Frobisher L.

ALBERTA

SASKATCHEWAN

Fort St. John

Peace River

Peace R.

Peter Pond L.

Lac Ile-à-la-Crosse

Dawson Creek

Utikuma L.

Lesser Slave L.

Primrose L.

Doré L.

BRITISH COLUMBIA

Grande Prairie

Smoky R.

Lac la Biche

Athabasca

Cold L.

Beaver R.

Prince George

Fraser R.

Fort Saskatchewan

North Saskatchewan R.

Hinton

Edmonton

Vegreville

Lloydminster

Drayton Valley

Camrose

Wainwright

North Battleford

Jasper

Wetaskiwin

Battle R.

Ponoka

Lacombe

Quesnel L.

Rocky Mountain House

Red Deer

Red Deer R.

Saskatchewan R.

Kicking Horse Pass

Drumheller

Trans-Canada Highway

Banff

Calgary

Bow R.

Turner Valley

Trans-Canada Highway

High River

South Saskatchewan R.

Medicine Hat

Claresholm

Kimberley

Crowsnest Pass

Fort Macleod

Kootenay L.

Kootenay R.

Oldman R.

Lethbridge

Cranbrook

Pincher Creek

Milk R.

UNITED STATES

LEGEND

- ⊙ Provincial Capitals
- ⊛ Major Cities
- • Other Cities and Towns
- ⟿ Power Sites
- ✈ Major Airports
- ⟿ Major Roads
- ～ Principal Railways
- –·– Provincial Boundaries
- — International Boundaries

Kilometres
0 50 100 150 200
Scale

Alberta
LANDFORMS—Relief

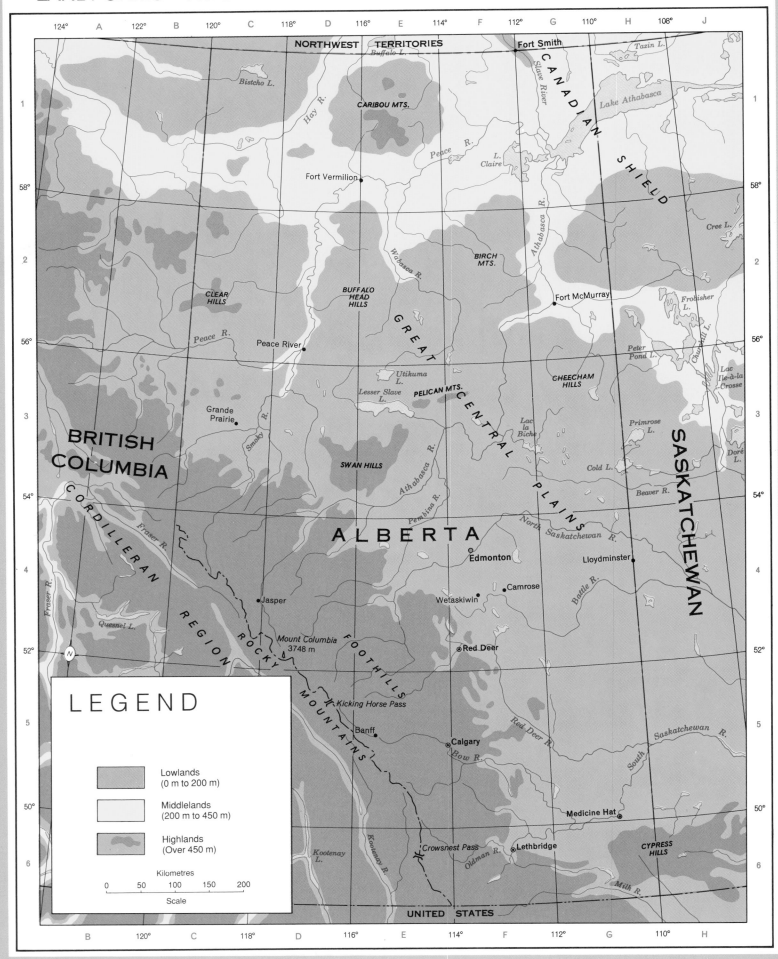

NORTHWEST TERRITORIES

Fort Smith

Buffalo L.

Tazin L.

Slave River

Bistcho L.

CARIBOU MTS.

Hay R.

Peace R.

Lake Athabasca

C A N A D I A N   S H I E L D

L. Claire

58°

Fort Vermilion

Cree L.

Athabasca R.

BIRCH MTS.

Wabasca R.

Frobisher L.

CLEAR HILLS

BUFFALO HEAD HILLS

Fort McMurray

56°

Peace R.

Peace River

G R E A T

Utikuma L.

Lesser Slave L.

PELICAN MTS.

Peter Pond L.

CHEECHAM HILLS

Churchill R.

Lac Ile-à-la-Crosse

Grande Prairie

Smoky R.

C E N T R A L

Lac la Biche

Primrose L.

Doré L.

BRITISH COLUMBIA

SWAN HILLS

Athabasca R.

P L A I N S

Cold L.

Beaver R.

54°

CORDILLERAN

Fraser R.

Pembina R.

A L B E R T A

North Saskatchewan R.

SASKATCHEWAN

Edmonton

Lloydminster

Fraser R.

REGION

Camrose

Battle R.

Jasper

Wetaskiwin

Quesnel L.

52°

Mount Columbia 3748 m

FOOTHILLS

Red Deer

ROCKY

Kicking Horse Pass

LEGEND

MOUNTAINS

Banff

Calgary

Red Deer R.

South Saskatchewan R.

Bow R.

Lowlands (0 m to 200 m)

Middlelands (200 m to 450 m)

50°

Medicine Hat

Highlands (Over 450 m)

Kootenay L.

Crowsnest Pass

Lethbridge

CYPRESS HILLS

Kootenay R.

Oldman R.

Kilometres

0   50   100   150   200

Scale

Milk R.

UNITED STATES

Alberta
FARMING

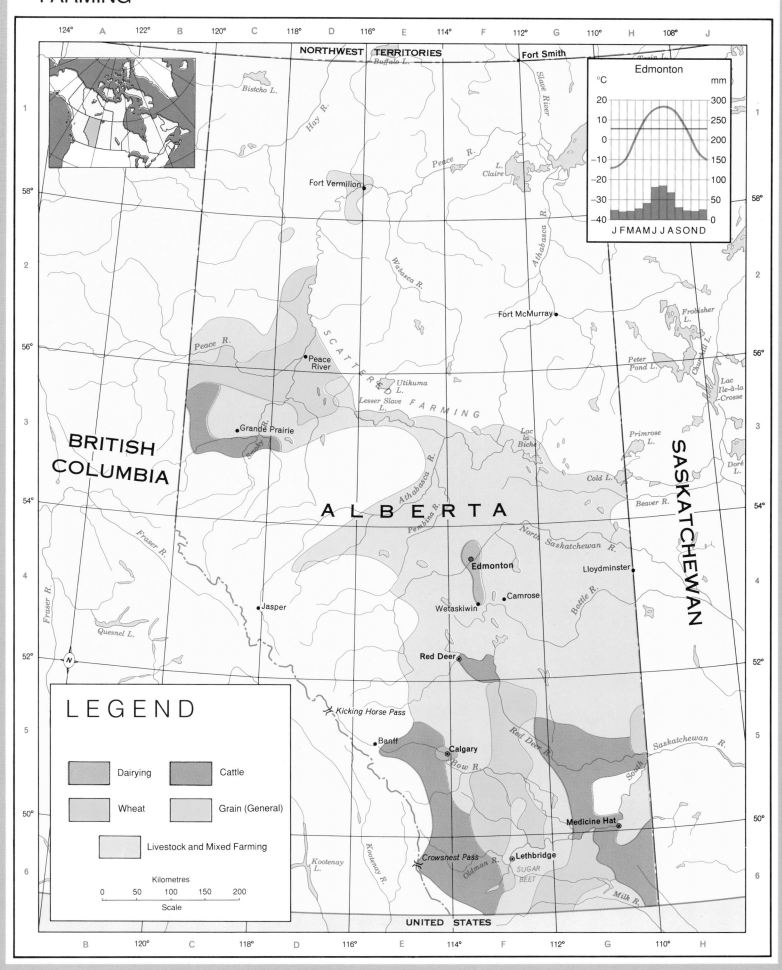

NORTHWEST TERRITORIES
Fort Smith
Buffalo L.
Bistcho L.
Hay R.
Slave River
Peace R.
L. Claire
Fort Vermilion
Athabasca R.

Edmonton
°C / mm
20 / 300
10 / 250
0 / 200
-10 / 150
-20 / 100
-30 / 50
-40 / 0
J F M A M J J A S O N D

Fort McMurray
Frobisher L.
Peace R.
Peace River
Utikuma L.
Lesser Slave L.
SCATTERED FARMING
Peter Pond L.
Churchill L.
Lac Ile-à-la-Crosse

BRITISH COLUMBIA
Smoky R.
Grande Prairie
Lac la Biche
Primrose L.
Doré L.

Fraser R.
Athabasca R.
ALBERTA
Cold L.
Beaver R.
SASKATCHEWAN

Pembina R.
North Saskatchewan R.
Edmonton
Lloydminster
Camrose
Battle R.
Jasper
Wetaskiwin

Quesnel L.
Red Deer

Kicking Horse Pass

LEGEND

	Dairying		Cattle
	Wheat		Grain (General)

Livestock and Mixed Farming

Banff
Calgary
Bow R.
Red Deer R.
Saskatchewan R.
Medicine Hat

Kilometres
0   50   100   150   200
Scale

Kootenay L.
Kootenay R.
Crowsnest Pass
Oldman R.
Lethbridge
SUGAR BEET
Milk R.

UNITED STATES

Alberta
MINING and INDUSTRIES

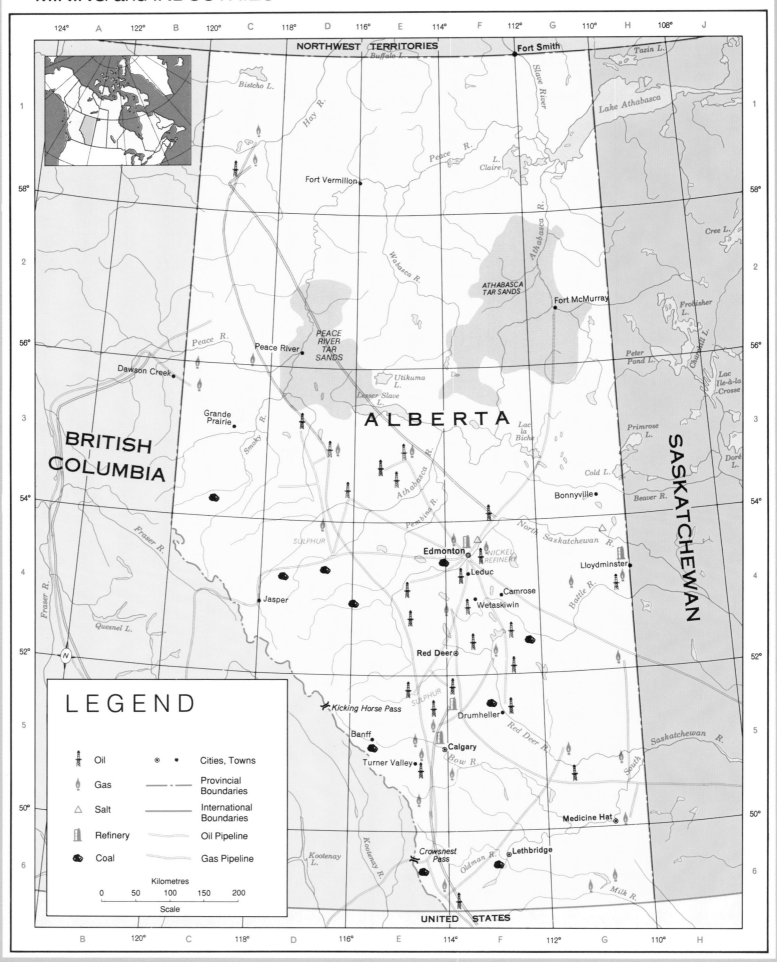

NORTHWEST TERRITORIES

Fort Smith

Tazin L.

Buffalo L.

Bistcho L.

Lake Athabasca

Slave River

Hay R.

Cree L.

Peace R.

L. Claire

Fort Vermilion

ATHABASCA TAR SANDS

Wabasca R.

Fort McMurray

Frobisher L.

Athabasca R.

Peter Pond L.

PEACE RIVER TAR SANDS

Utikuma L.

Peace R.

Peace River

Lac Ile-à-la-Crosse

Dawson Creek

Lesser Slave L.

ALBERTA

Lac la Biche

Primrose L.

Grande Prairie

Smoky R.

BRITISH COLUMBIA

Doré L.

Cold L.

Bonnyville

Beaver R.

Athabasca R.

Fraser R.

SULPHUR

Pembina R.

SASKATCHEWAN

North Saskatchewan R.

Edmonton

NICKEL REFINERY

Leduc

Lloydminster

Fraser R.

Jasper

Camrose

Wetaskiwin

Battle R.

Quesnel L.

Red Deer

N

Kicking Horse Pass

SULPHUR

Drumheller

Red Deer R.

LEGEND

Banff

Saskatchewan R.

Calgary

Turner Valley

Bow R.

South Saskatchewan R.

	Oil		Cities, Towns
	Gas		Provincial Boundaries
	Salt		International Boundaries
	Refinery		Oil Pipeline
	Coal		Gas Pipeline

Medicine Hat

Kootenay L.

Crowsnest Pass

Lethbridge

Kilometres

Kootenay R.

Oldman R.

0   50   100   150   200

Milk R.

Scale

UNITED STATES

British Columbia
TRANSPORTATION

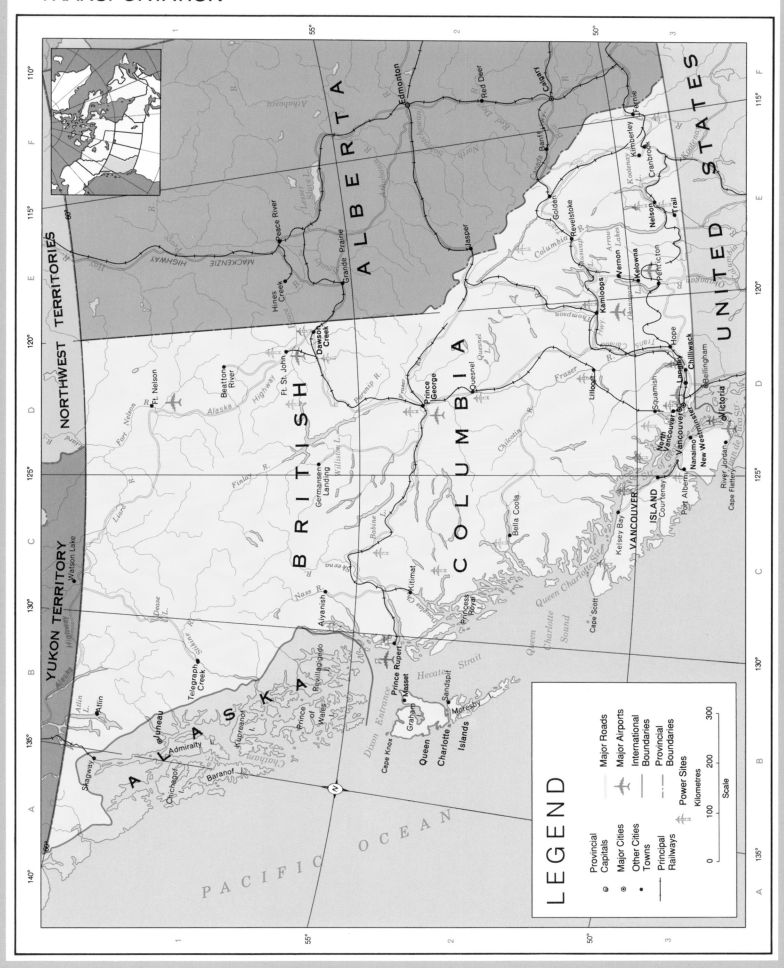

NORTHWEST TERRITORIES

YUKON TERRITORY

ALBERTA

BRITISH COLUMBIA

ALASKA

UNITED STATES

VANCOUVER ISLAND

PACIFIC OCEAN

Edmonton
Red Deer
Calgary
Banff
Fernie
Kimberley
Cranbrook
Golden
Revelstoke
Nelson
Trail
Jasper
Vernon
Kelowna
Penticton
Kamloops
Hope
Chilliwack
Bellingham
Langley
Squamish
Lillooet
Vancouver
North Vancouver
New Westminster
Victoria
Nanaimo
Port Alberni
Courtenay
Kelsey Bay
River Jordan
Cape Flattery
Quesnel
Prince George
Bella Coola
Cape Scott
Kitimat
Aiyanish
Prince Rupert
Masset
Sandspit
Moresby
Graham
Queen Charlotte Islands
Cape Knox
Germansen Landing
Ft. St. John
Dawson Creek
Beatton River
Ft. Nelson
Peace River
Hines Creek
Grande Prairie
Watson Lake
Telegraph Creek
Atlin
Juneau
Skagway
Chichagof
Admiralty
Baranof
Kupreanof
Revillagigedo
Prince of Wales

Peace River
Athabasca R.
Lesser Slave L.
North Saskatchewan R.
South Saskatchewan R.
Red Deer R.
Kootenay L.
Arrow L.
Shuswap L.
Columbia R.
Thompson R.
Fraser R.
Quesnel L.
Williston L.
Babine L.
Finlay R.
Parsnip R.
Nass R.
Skeena R.
Chilcotin R.
Liard R.
Dease L.
Stikine R.
Fort Nelson R.
Atlin L.
Queen Charlotte Sound
Queen Charlotte Str.
Hecate Strait
Dixon Entrance
Douglas Ch.
Princess Royal

Alaska Highway
Mackenzie Highway
Hart Highway
Trans Canada Hwy

LEGEND

Symbol	Meaning	Symbol	Meaning
◉	Provincial Capitals	—	Major Roads
⊙	Major Cities	✈	Major Airports
•	Other Cities Towns	—	International Boundaries
—	Principal Railways	⋯	Provincial Boundaries
		■	Power Sites

Kilometres
0   100   200   300
Scale

British Columbia
LANDFORMS—Relief

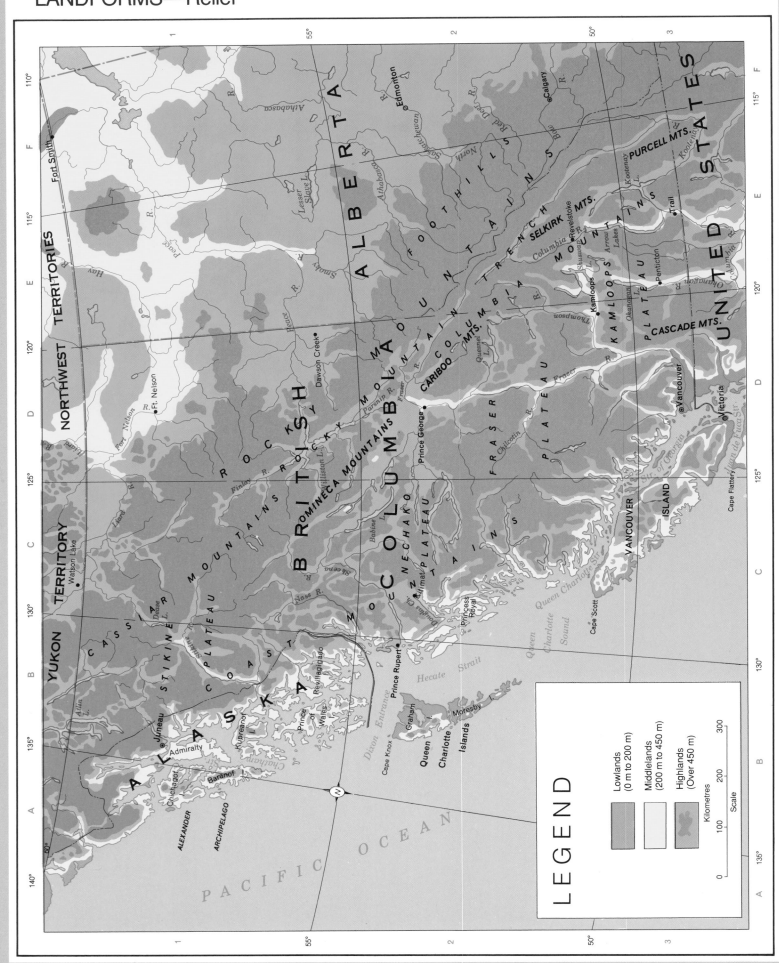

LEGEND

Lowlands (0 m to 200 m)

Middlelands (200 m to 450 m)

Highlands (Over 450 m)

Scale

Kilometres

0   100   200   300

British Columbia
FARMING

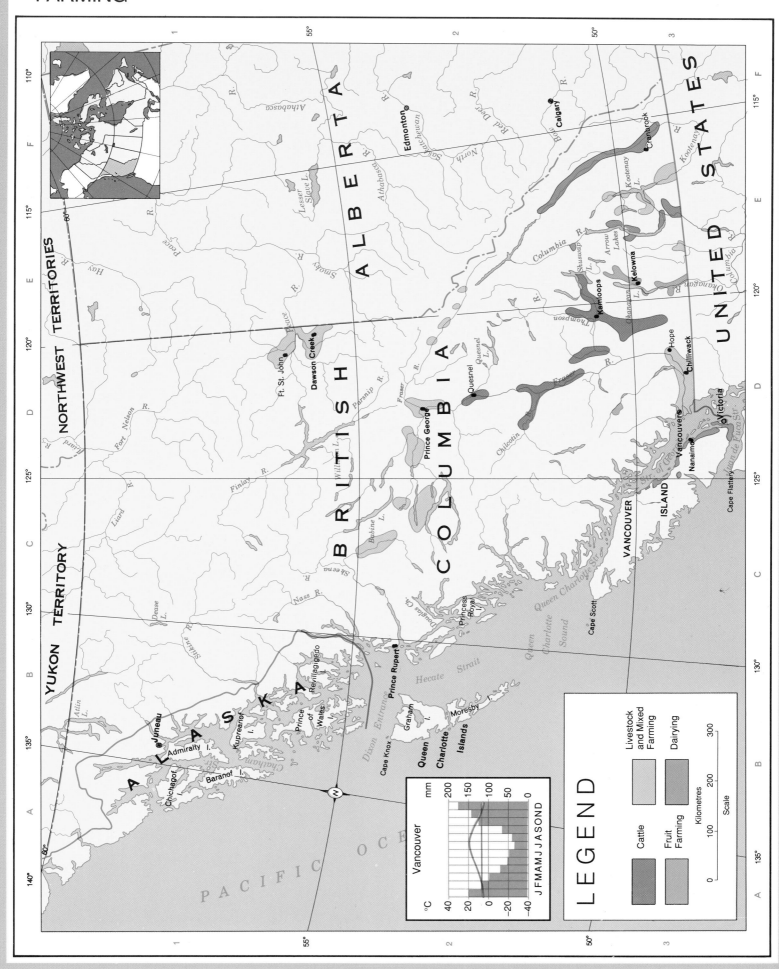

PACIFIC OCEAN

LEGEND

Cattle	Livestock and Mixed Farming
Fruit Farming	Dairying

Kilometres

0   100   200   300

Scale

Vancouver

°C mm
40 200
    150
20 100
0   50
-20 0
-40

J F M A M J J A S O N D

British Columbia
MINING and INDUSTRIES

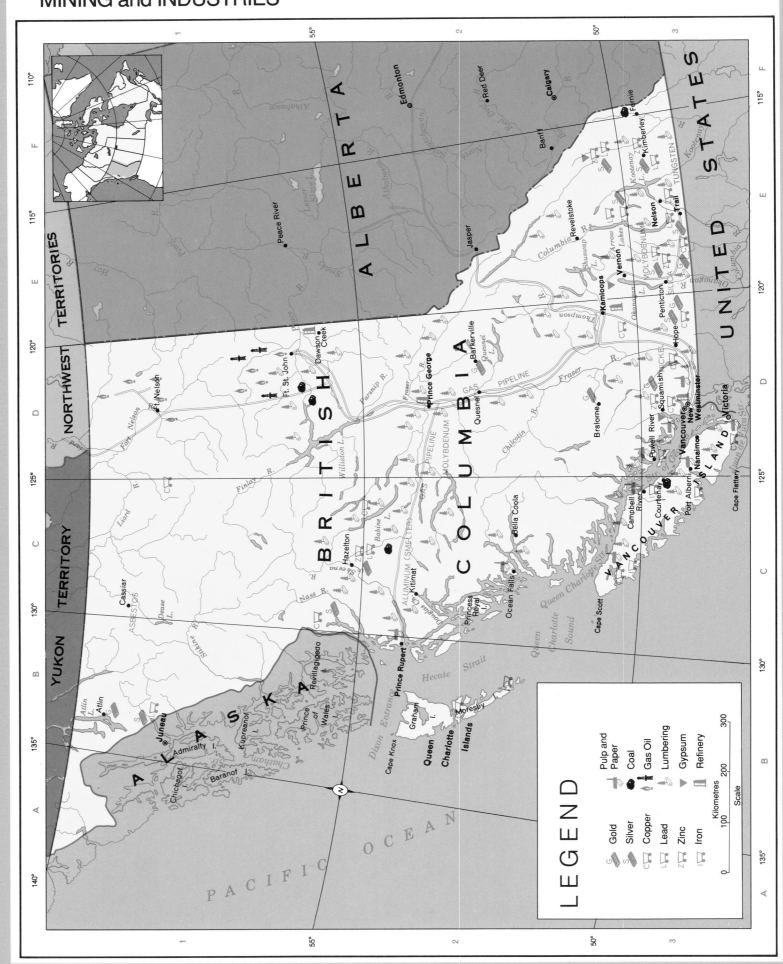

LEGEND

G Gold
S Silver
Cu Copper
Pb Lead
Zn Zinc
Fe Iron

Pulp and Paper
Coal
Gas Oil
Lumbering
Gypsum
Refinery

Scale
Kilometres
0   100   200   300

The St. Lawrence Seaway System

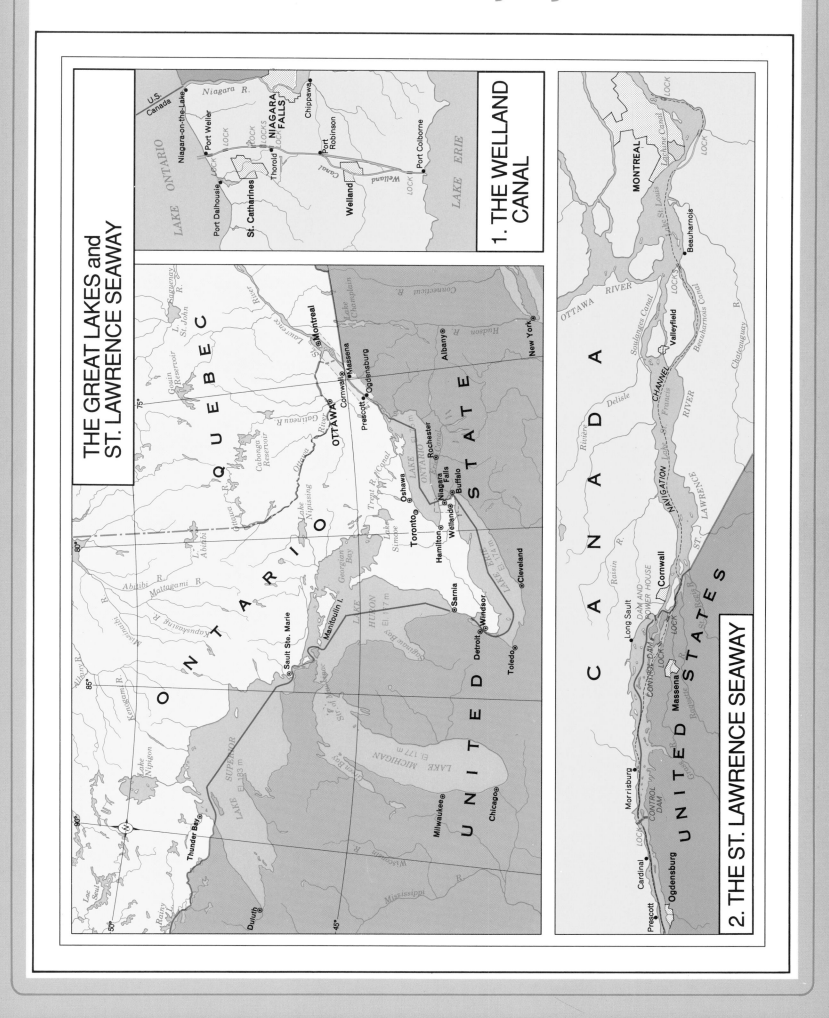

1. THE WELLAND CANAL

THE GREAT LAKES and ST. LAWRENCE SEAWAY

2. THE ST. LAWRENCE SEAWAY

Canada
THE NORTHLAND

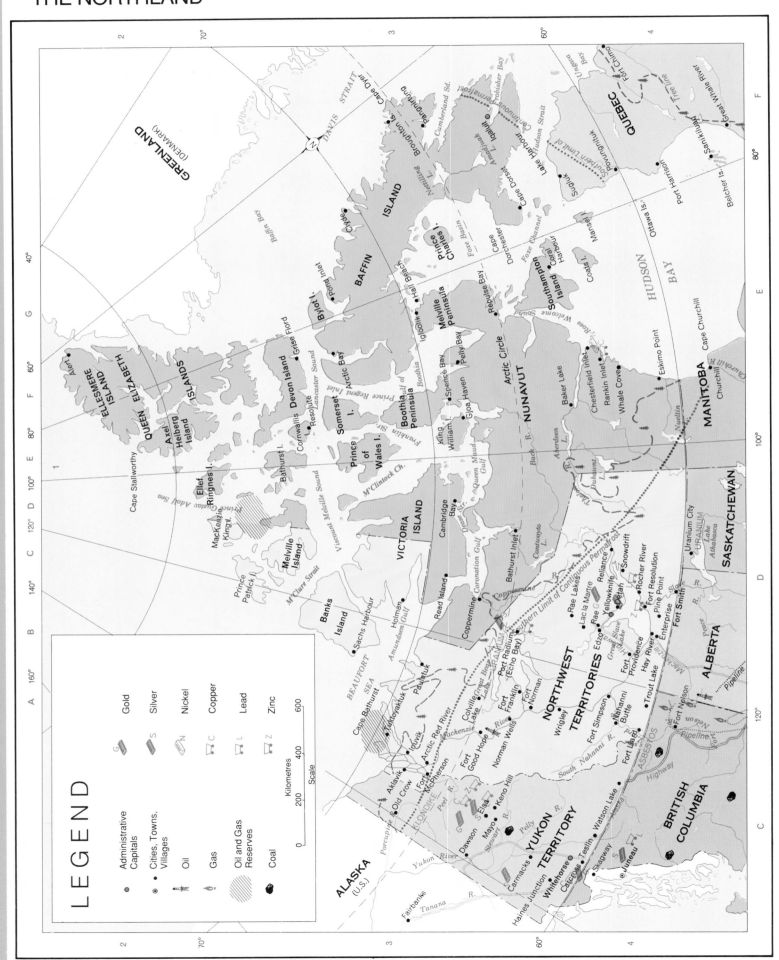

LEGEND

- ● Administrative Capitals
- ● Cities, Towns, Villages
- Oil
- Gas
- Oil and Gas Reserves
- Coal

- G Gold
- S Silver
- N Nickel
- C Copper
- L Lead
- Z Zinc

Scale

Kilometres

0   200   400   600

GREENLAND (DENMARK)

DAVIS STRAIT

Cape Dyer

BAFFIN ISLAND

QUEEN ELIZABETH ISLANDS

ELLESMERE ISLAND

Alert

Cape Stallworthy

Axel Heiberg Island

Ellef Ringnes I.

Prince Gustav Adolf Sea

MacKenzie King I.

Melville Island

Prince Patrick I.

Banks Island

Sachs Harbour

Holman

BEAUFORT SEA

Cape Bathurst

Tuktoyaktuk

Paulatuk

Devon Island

Grise Fiord

Bylot I.

Pond Inlet

Arctic Bay

Somerset I.

Bathurst I.

Cornwallis I.

Resolute

Lancaster Sound

Prince of Wales I.

Boothia Peninsula

M'Clintock Ch.

VICTORIA ISLAND

Read Island

Cambridge Bay

Coppermine

Coronation Gulf

Bathurst Inlet

Contwoyto L.

Clyde

Panguirtung

Broughton Is.

Frobisher Bay

Iqaluit

Cape Dorset

Prince Charles I.

Foxe Basin

Hall Beach

Igloolik

Melville Peninsula

Repulse Bay

Pelly Bay

Spence Bay

Gjoa Haven

King William I.

Franklin Str.

Gulf of Boothia

Prince Regent Inlet

Cumberland Sd.

Amadjuak L.

Lake Harbour

Hudson Strait

Foxe Channel

Cape Dorchester

NUNAVUT

Arctic Circle

Welcome Sound

Southampton Island

Coats I.

Coral Harbour

Mansel I.

HUDSON BAY

Sugluk

Povungnituk

Continuous Permafrost

QUEBEC

Fort Chimo

Ungava Bay

Tree Line

Great Whale River

Belcher Is.

Port Harrison

Ottawa Is.

Baker Lake

Aberdeen L.

Back R.

Chesterfield Inlet

Rankin Inlet

Whale Cove

Eskimo Point

Cape Churchill

Churchill

MANITOBA

Churchill R.

Nueltin L.

Dubawnt L.

Thelon R.

Southern Limit of Continuous Permafrost

Southern Limit of Contiguous Permafrost

FRANKLIN

Port Radium (Echo Bay)

Great Bear Lake

Fort Franklin

Fort Norman

Norman Wells

Good Hope

Fort Good Hope

Colville Lake

Arctic Red River

Fort McPherson

Inuvik

Aklavik

Old Crow

Porcupine R.

Peel R.

Mackenzie R.

Fort Providence

Fort Simpson

Wrigley

Nahanni Butte

South Nahanni R.

Fort Liard

Coppermine R.

Rae Lakes

Rae

Lac la Martre

Edzo

Yellowknife

Detah

Rae G

Great Slave Lake

Snowdrift

Reliance

Rocher River

Fort Resolution

Pine Point

Enterprise

Hay River

Trout Lake

Fort Smith

NORTHWEST TERRITORIES

SASKATCHEWAN

Uranium City

Lake Athabasca

URANIUM

Fort Nelson

Nelson R.

Pipeline

ALBERTA

Peace R.

Slave R.

Mackenzie R.

ASBESTOS

Highway

BRITISH COLUMBIA

Watson Lake

Testin

Caicross

Whitehorse

Skagway

Juneau

Haines Junction

Carmacks

Carcross

Keno Hill

Mayo

Elsa

Dawson

Stewart R.

Pelly R.

Yukon R.

YUKON TERRITORY

KLONDIKE

ALASKA (U.S.)

Fairbanks

Tanana R.

Yukon River

Amundsen Gulf

M'Clure Strait

Viscount Melville Sound

Queen Maud Gulf

Baffin Bay

N

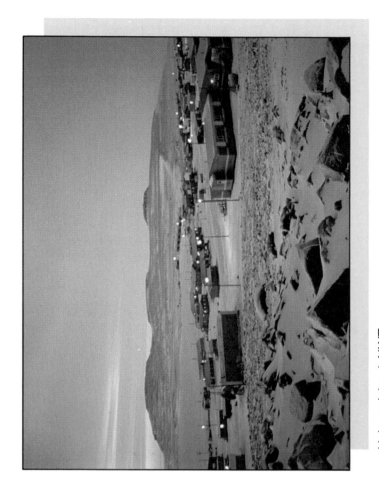

Holman Island, NWT

Whitehorse, YT

Pond Inlet, Nunavut

Yellowknife

Whitehorse

The United States
POLITICAL DIVISIONS—(excluding Alaska and Hawaii)

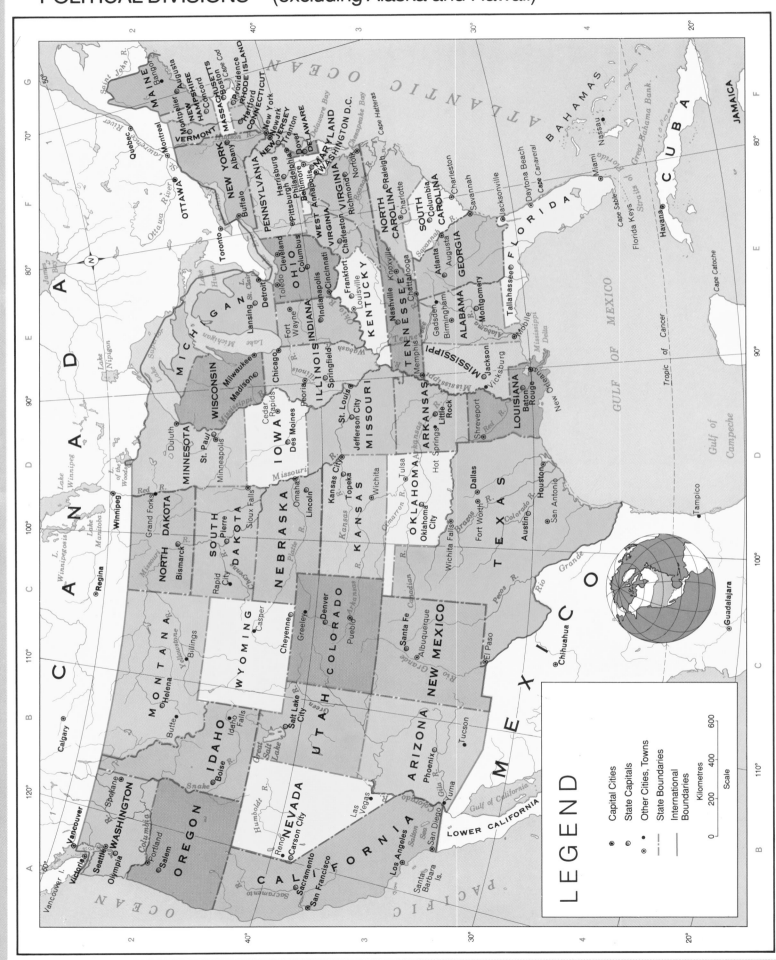

LEGEND

- ● Capital Cities
- ◉ State Capitals
- • Other Cities, Towns
- –·–· State Boundaries
- —— International Boundaries

Kilometres
0   200   400   600
Scale

Houston, TX

New York, NY

San Francisco, CA

The United States
LANDFORMS—Relief

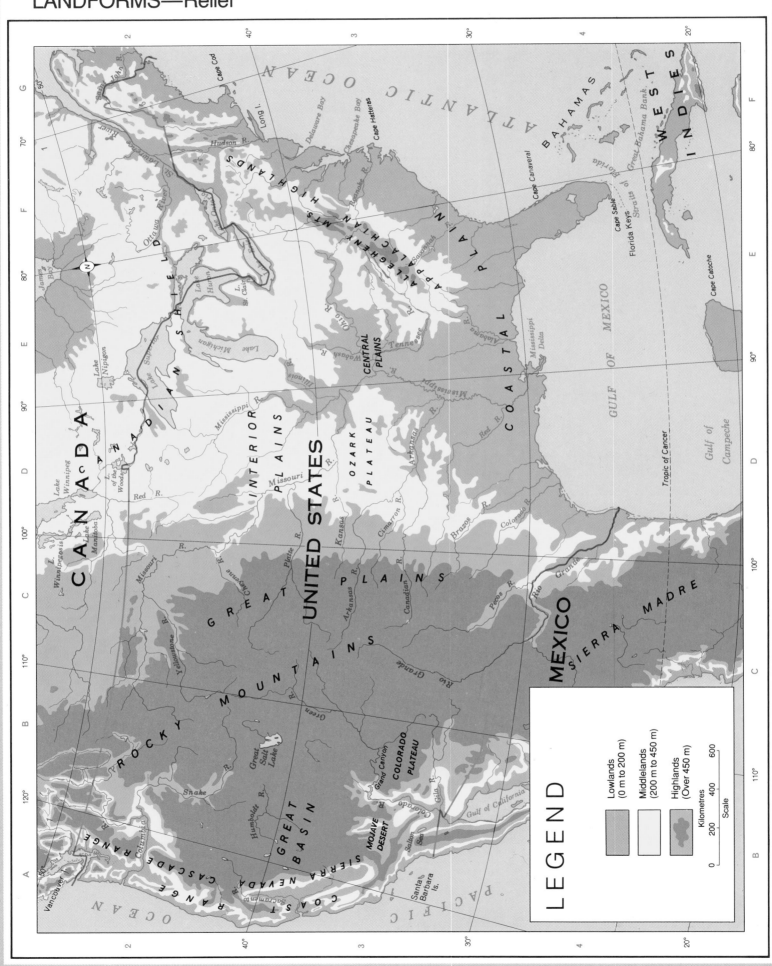

LEGEND

Lowlands (0 m to 200 m)

Middlelands (200 m to 450 m)

Highlands (Over 450 m)

Kilometres

Scale

0   200   400   600

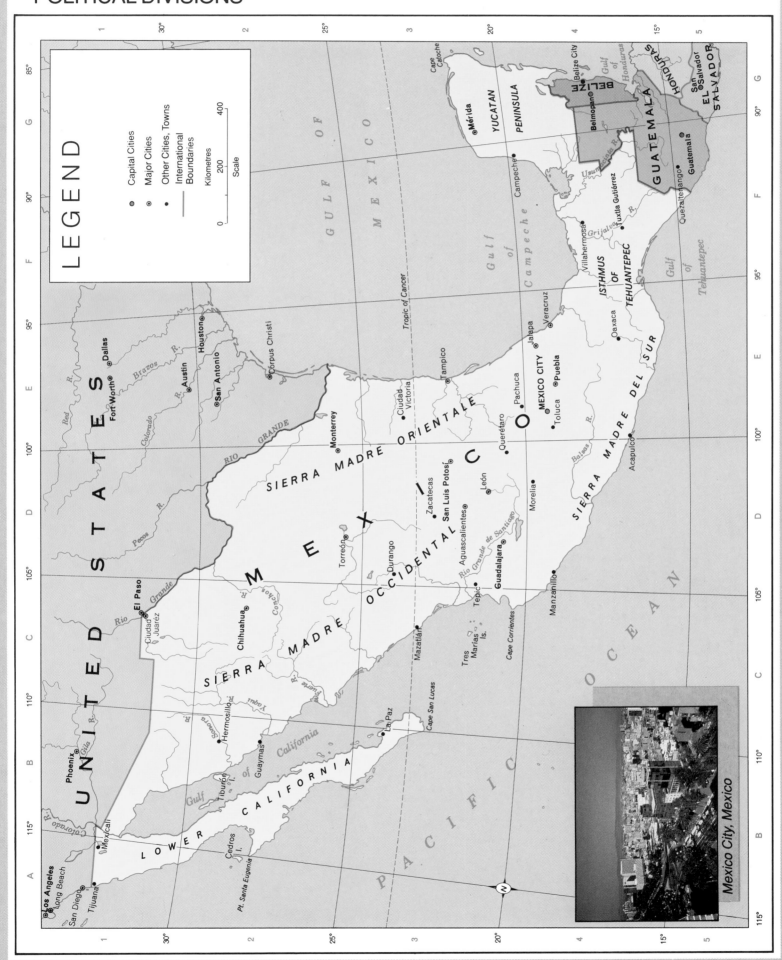

Mexico
POLITICAL DIVISIONS

LEGEND

- Capital Cities
- Major Cities
- Other Cities, Towns
- International Boundaries

Scale

Kilometres
400
200
0

UNITED STATES

Los Angeles
Long Beach
San Diego
Tijuana
Mexicali
Phoenix
El Paso
Ciudad Juárez
Chihuahua
Hermosillo
Guaymas
La Paz
Cedros I.
Pt. Santa Eugenia
Cape San Lucas

Dallas
Fort Worth
Austin
San Antonio
Houston
Corpus Christi
Monterrey
Torreón
Durango
Mazatlán
Tres Marías Is.
Cape Corrientes
Manzanillo
Tepic
Guadalajara
Aguascalientes
León
Zacatecas
San Luis Potosí
Querétaro
Morelia
Toluca
MEXICO CITY
Puebla
Pachuca
Acapulco
Ciudad Victoria
Tampico
Veracruz
Jalapa
Oaxaca
Villahermosa
Tuxtla Gutiérrez
Campeche
Mérida
Cape Catoche

MEXICO

SIERRA MADRE ORIENTALE
SIERRA MADRE OCCIDENTAL
SIERRA MADRE DEL SUR

LOWER CALIFORNIA
Gulf of California
Tiburón

RIO GRANDE

Tropic of Cancer

GULF OF MEXICO
Gulf of Campeche

YUCATAN PENINSULA

BELIZE
Belize City
Belmopan
Gulf of Honduras

GUATEMALA
Guatemala
Quezaltenango
HONDURAS
San Salvador
EL SALVADOR

ISTHMUS OF TEHUANTEPEC
Gulf of Tehuantepec

PACIFIC OCEAN

N

Mexico City, Mexico

Central America
POLITICAL DIVISIONS

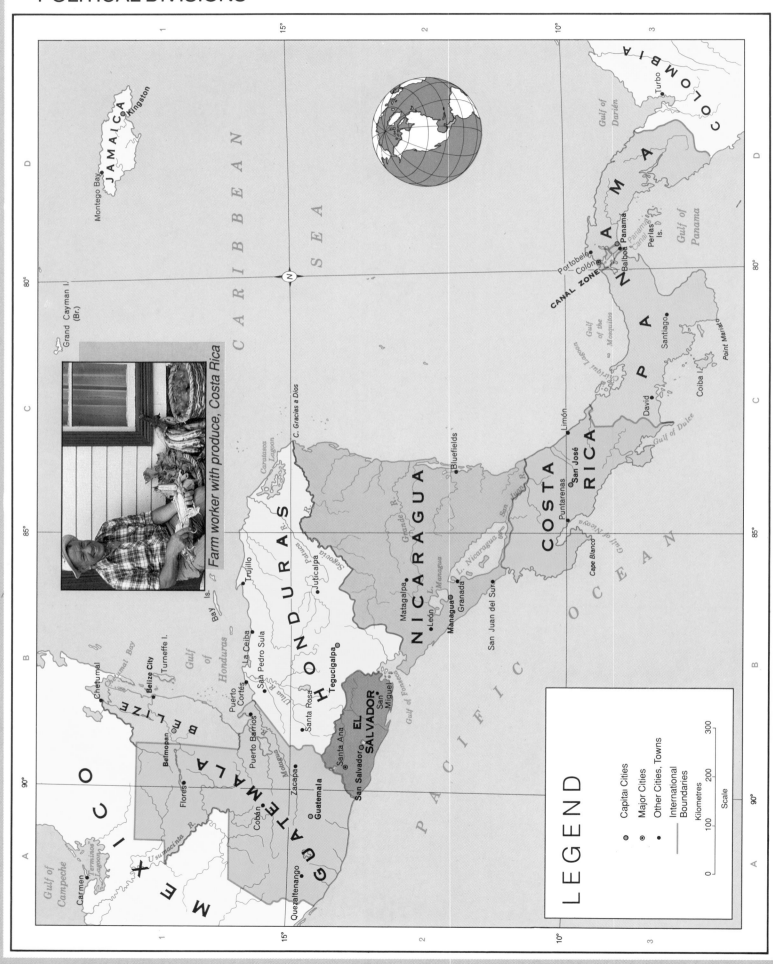

Farm worker with produce, Costa Rica

JAMAICA
Kingston
Montego Bay

CARIBBEAN SEA

COLOMBIA
Turbo
Gulf of Darién

PANAMA

Grand Cayman I. (Br.)

Gulf of Panama
Perlas Is.
Panamá
Balboa
Colón
Portobelo
CANAL ZONE
Panama Canal

Gulf of the Mosquitos

Santiago
David
Point Mariato
Coiba I.

Gulf of Dulce

COSTA RICA
Limón
San José
Puntarenas

Cape Blanco
Gulf of Nicoya

RICA

Bluefields

San Juan del Sur

NICARAGUA
Matagalpa
León
Managua
Granada
L. Managua
L. Nicaragua
San Juan R.

C. Gracias a Dios

Caratasca Lagoon

HONDURAS
Trujillo
Juticalpa
Tegucigalpa
Santa Rosa
La Ceiba
San Pedro Sula
Puerto Cortés
Patuca R.
Segovia R.
Ulúa R.

Gulf of Honduras
Turneffe I.
Bay Is.

Belize City
Chetumal
BELIZE
Belmopan
Puerto Barrios

GUATEMALA
Flores
Cobán
Zacapa
Guatemala
Quezaltenango
Motagua R.
Usumacinta R.

EL SALVADOR
Santa Ana
San Salvador
San Miguel
Gulf of Fonseca

MEXICO
Carmen
Terminos Lagoon
Gulf of Campeche
Usumacinta R.

PACIFIC OCEAN

LEGEND

- ● Capital Cities
- ◎ Major Cities
- • Other Cities, Towns
- — International Boundaries

Scale

Kilometres

0   100   200   300

The Caribbean Islands
POLITICAL DIVISIONS

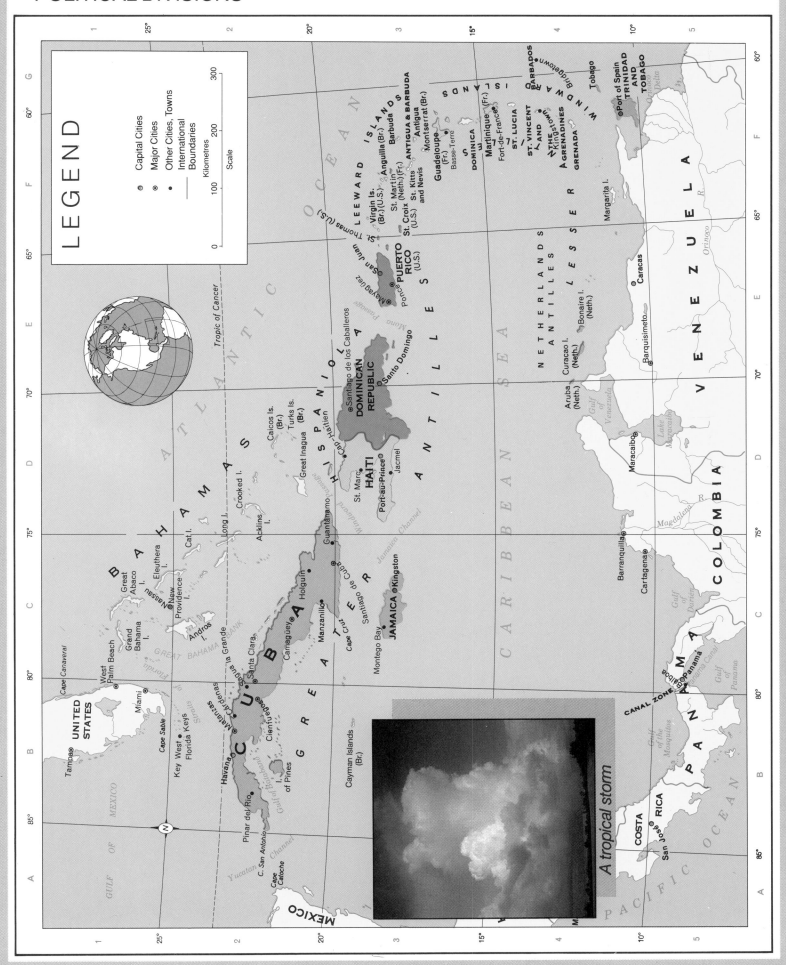

LEGEND

- Capital Cities
- Major Cities
- Other Cities, Towns
- International Boundaries

Kilometres

Scale

0   100   200   300

Tropic of Cancer

ATLANTIC OCEAN

GULF OF MEXICO

UNITED STATES

Cape Canaveral

West Palm Beach

Miami

Tampa

Key West

Cape Sable

Florida Keys

Florida Strait

Grand Bahama I.

Great Abaco I.

BAHAMAS

Nassau

New Providence I.

Eleuthera I.

Andros I.

Cat I.

Long I.

Crooked I.

Acklins I.

GREAT BAHAMA BANK

Pinar del Rio

Havana

Matanzas

Cárdenas

Sabana la Grande

Santa Clara

Cienfuegos

C U B A

Gulf of Batabanó

Isle of Pines

Yucatán Channel

C. San Antonio

Cape Catoche

MÉXICO

Cayman Islands (Br.)

Camagüey

Manzanillo

Holguín

Cape Cruz

Santiago de Cuba

Guantánamo

Montego Bay

JAMAICA

Kingston

Great Inagua

Caicos Is. (Br.)

Turks Is. (Br.)

Windward Passage

Cap-Haïtien

HISPANIOLA

Santiago de los Caballeros

DOMINICAN REPUBLIC

Santo Domingo

St. Marc

HAITI

Port-au-Prince

Jacmel

Jamaica Channel

G R E A T E R   A N T I L L E S

Mona Passage

Mayagüez

San Juan

Ponce

PUERTO RICO (U.S.)

Virgin Is. (Br.) (U.S.)

St. Thomas (U.S.)

St. Croix (U.S.)

St. Martin (Fr.)

Anguilla (Br.)

St. Kitts and Nevis

Montserrat (Br.)

Antigua

ANTIGUA & BARBUDA

Barbuda

LEEWARD ISLANDS

Guadeloupe (Fr.)

Basse-Terre

DOMINICA

Martinique (Fr.)

Fort-de-France

ST. LUCIA

ST. VINCENT AND THE GRENADINES

Kingstown

Barbados

Bridgetown

BARBADOS

GRENADA

Tobago

Port of Spain

TRINIDAD AND TOBAGO

W I N D W A R D   I S L A N D S

L E S S E R   A N T I L L E S

Margarita I.

NETHERLANDS ANTILLES

Curaçao I. (Neth.)

Bonaire I. (Neth.)

Aruba (Neth.)

Gulf of Venezuela

Lake Maracaibo

CARIBBEAN SEA

Barranquilla

Cartagena

Gulf of Darién

Gulf of the Mosquitos

PANAMÁ

Balboa

Panamá

CANAL ZONE

Gulf of Panama

COSTA RICA

San José

PACIFIC OCEAN

COLOMBIA

VENEZUELA

Caracas

Barquisimeto

Maracaibo

Orinoco R.

Magdalena R.

A tropical storm

South America
POLITICAL DIVISIONS

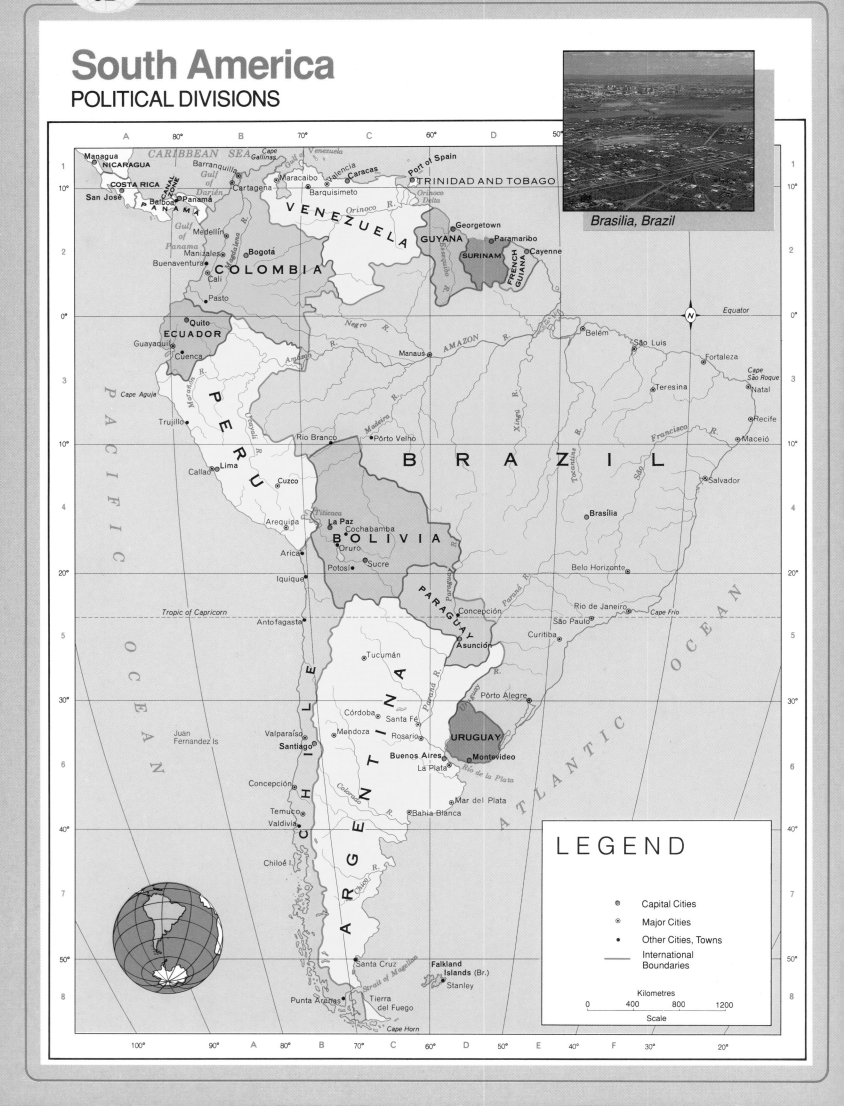

Brasilia, Brazil

CARIBBEAN SEA
Cape Gallinas
Gulf of Venezuela

Managua
NICARAGUA
COSTA RICA
San José
Balboa
Panamá
PANAMA
CANAL ZONE
Gulf of Darién
Barranquilla
Gulf of
Cartagena
Maracaibo
Valencia
Caracas
Barquisimeto
Port of Spain
TRINIDAD AND TOBAGO
Orinoco Delta

V E N E Z U E L A
Orinoco R.
Essequibo R.
GUYANA
Georgetown
SURINAM
Paramaribo
Cayenne
FRENCH GUIANA

Medellín
Manizales
Bogotá
Buenaventura
Cali
C O L O M B I A
Pasto
Magdalena R.

Negro R.

Quito
ECUADOR
Guayaquil
Cuenca
Amazon R.
Marañón R.
Ucayali R.
AMAZON
Manaus
Belém
São Luis
Fortaleza
Cape São Roque
Natal
Equator

Cape Aguja
P E R U
Trujillo
Rio Branco
Pôrto Velho
Madeira R.
Teresina
Recife
Maceió

Callao
Lima
Cuzco
B R A Z I L
São Francisco R.
Salvador

Arequipa
Titicaca
La Paz
Cochabamba
B O L I V I A
Oruro
Arica
Potosí
Sucre
Xingú R.
Tocantins R.
Brasília
Belo Horizonte

Iquique
Antofagasta
Tropic of Capricorn
P A R A G U A Y
Concepción
Pilcomayo R.
Paraná R.
Rio de Janeiro
Cape Frio
São Paulo
Curitiba

Tucumán
Asunción
Paraná R.
R.
Pôrto Alegre
Uruguay R.

Juan Fernandez Is
Valparaíso
Mendoza
Córdoba
Santa Fé
Rosario
A R G E N T I N A
C H I L E
Santiago
Buenos Aires
La Plata
Río de la Plata
URUGUAY
Montevideo
Mar del Plata
Bahia Blanca

Concepción
Colorado R.
Temuco
Valdivia
Chiloé I.
Chuco R.

P A C I F I C   O C E A N
A T L A N T I C   O C E A N

Santa Cruz
Strait of Magellan
Punta Arenas
Tierra del Fuego
Cape Horn
Falkland Islands (Br.)
Stanley

LEGEND

- ● Capital Cities
- ◉ Major Cities
- • Other Cities, Towns
- — International Boundaries

Kilometres

0   400   800   1200

Scale

South America
LANDFORMS—Relief

CARIBBEAN SEA
Cape Gallinas
Gulf of Venezuela
Gulf of Darién
Gulf of Panama
Magdalena R.
LLANOS
Orinoco R.
Orinoco Delta
TRINIDAD AND TOBAGO
GUIANA HIGHLANDS
Essequibo R.
Negro R.
Equator
N
Amazon
AMAZON
R.
R.
Marañón R.
Cape Aguja
Ucayali R.
SELVAS
Madeira R.
Xingú R.
Tocantins R.
São Francisco R.
Cape São Roque
A
N
D
E
S
L. Titicaca
MATO GROSSO UPLAND
São
BRAZILIAN HIGHLANDS
Cape Frío
PLATEAU OF BOLIVIA
GRAN CHACO
Paraguay R.
Paraná R.
CAMPOS
Tropic of Capricorn
Uruguay R.
PACIFIC OCEAN
Juan Fernandez Is
Colorado
PAMPAS
Río de la Plata
ATLANTIC OCEAN
Chiloé I.
CHONOS ARCHIPELAGO
Chico
P A T A G O N I A
Strait of Magellan
Falkland Islands (Br.)
Tierra del Fuego
Cape Horn

LEGEND

Lowlands
(0 m to 200 m)

Middlelands
(200 m to 450 m)

Highlands
(Over 450 m)

Kilometres
0   400   800   1200
Scale

South America
TEMPERATURES—January and July

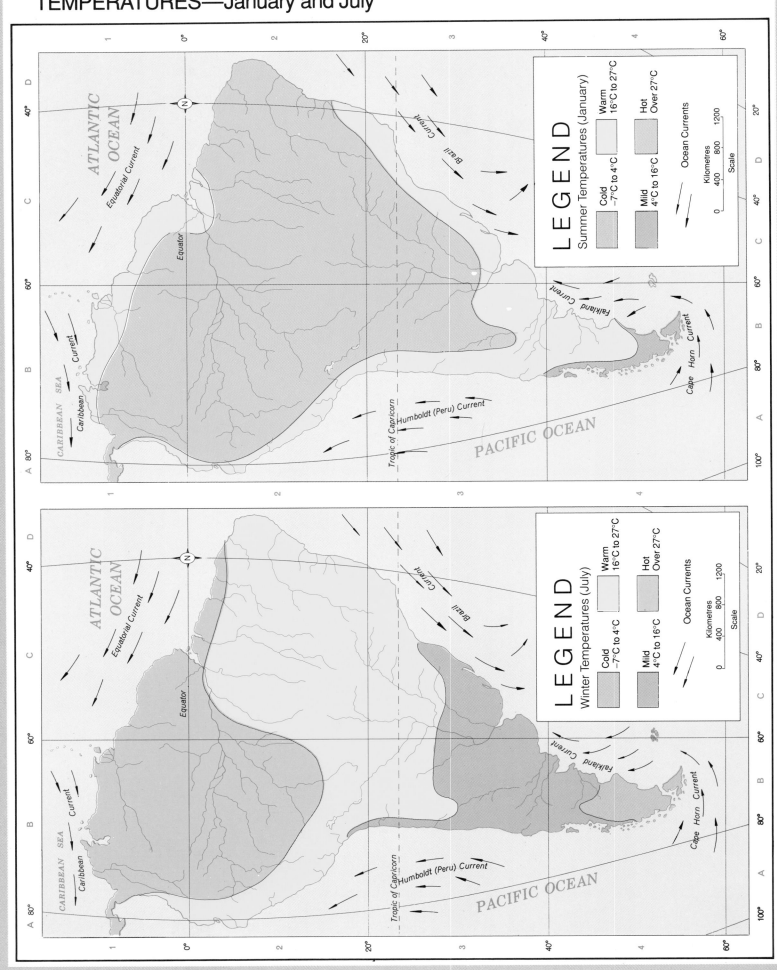

South America
ANNUAL RAINFALL and VEGETATION

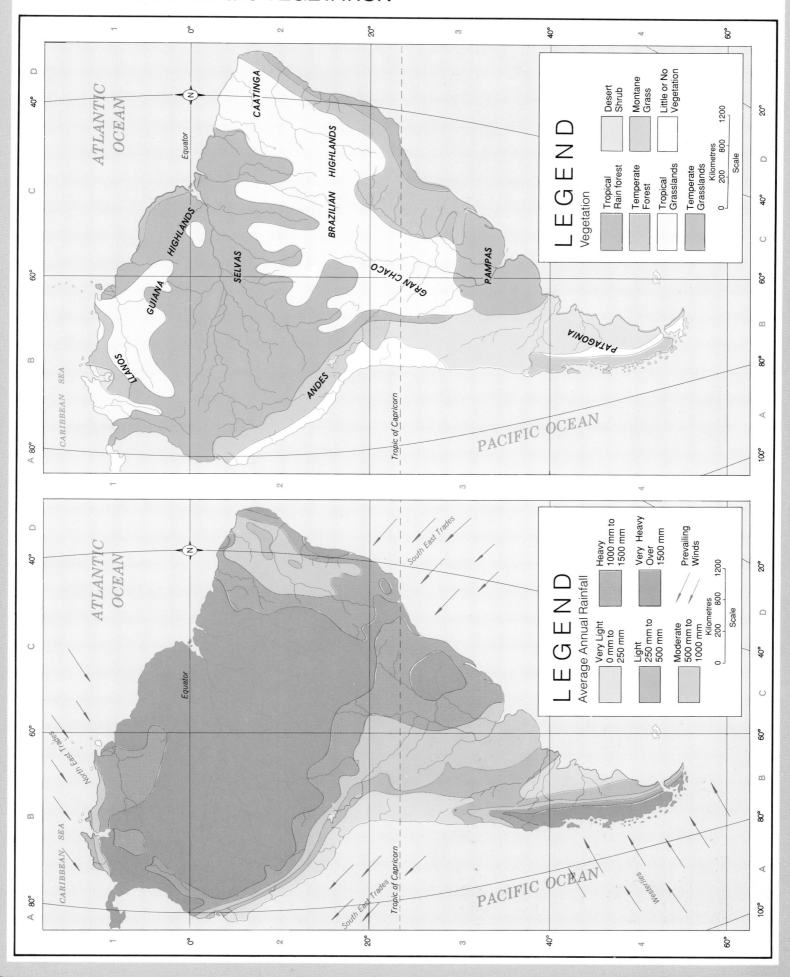

South America
RAIN FORESTS

South American rain forests, before and after clearing

Where Our Rain Forests Go

Somewhere in the world, 12 to 20 hectares of rain forest disappear every thirty minutes. Forty percent of the world's rain forests have already vanished. By the year 2000, some countries will have lost their entire forest area.

Yanomami Indians in the Amazon rain forest.

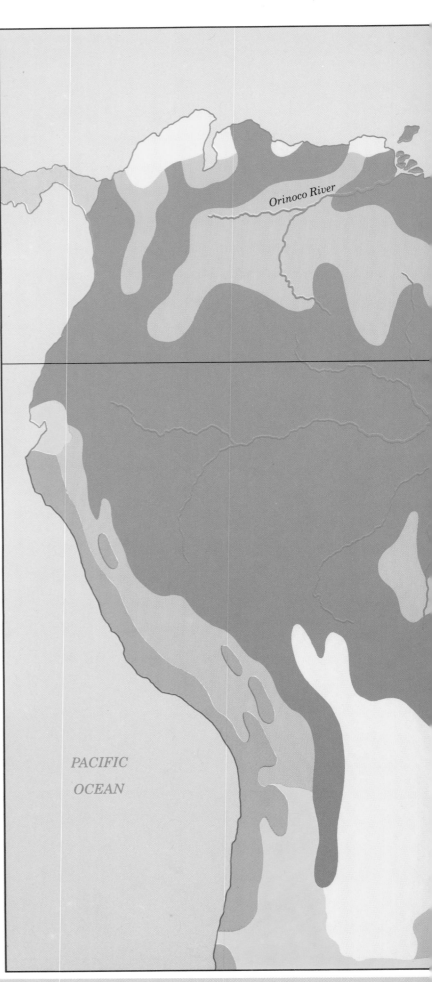

Orinoco River

PACIFIC OCEAN

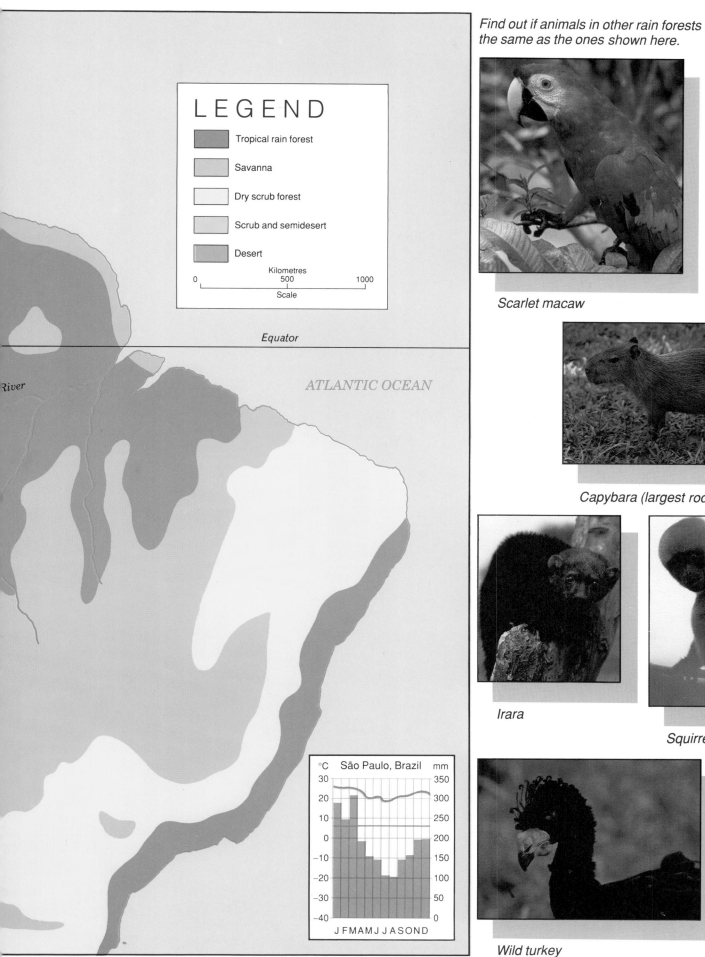

LEGEND

- Tropical rain forest
- Savanna
- Dry scrub forest
- Scrub and semidesert
- Desert

Kilometres
0   500   1000
Scale

Equator

River

ATLANTIC OCEAN

°C São Paulo, Brazil mm

J F M A M J J A S O N D

Find out if animals in other rain forests in the world are the same as the ones shown here.

Scarlet macaw

Capybara (largest rodent on Earth)

Irara

Squirrel monkey

Wild turkey

Africa
POLITICAL DIVISIONS

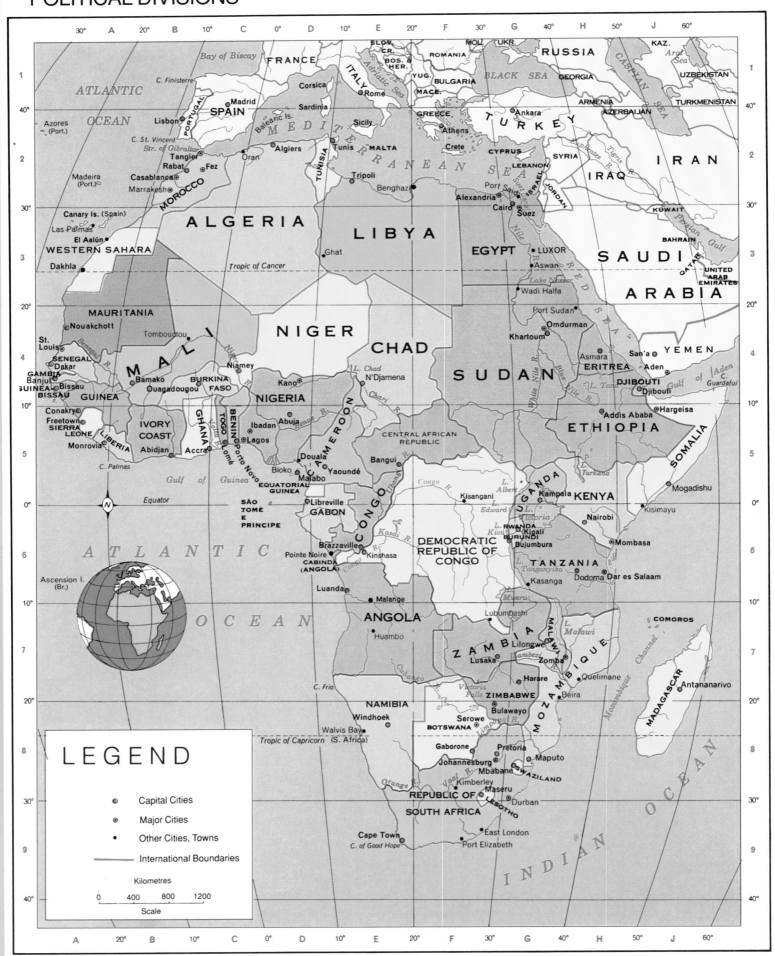

LEGEND

- ◉ Capital Cities
- ⊙ Major Cities
- • Other Cities, Towns
- — International Boundaries

Kilometres

0   400   800   1200

Scale

Nairobi, Kenya

Cape Town, South Africa

Luxor, Egypt

Algiers, Algeria

Africa
LANDFORMS—Relief

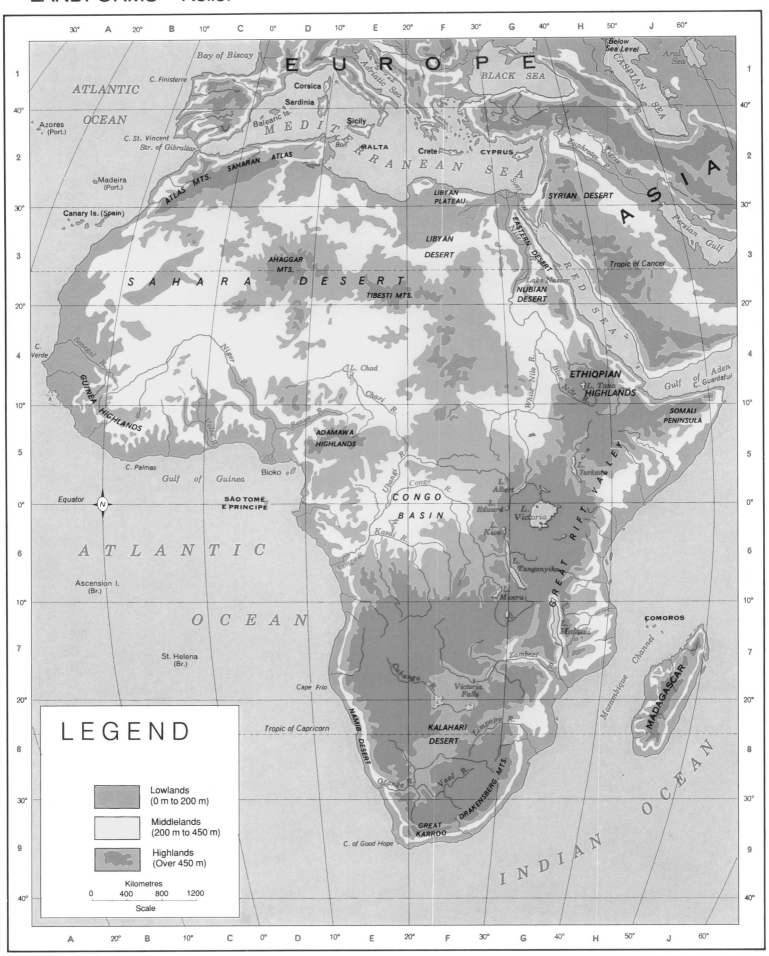

LEGEND

Lowlands
(0 m to 200 m)

Middlelands
(200 m to 450 m)

Highlands
(Over 450 m)

Kilometres
0   400   800   1200
Scale

Desert Record

The Sahara desert is the largest desert in the world with an area of over 8 million square kilometres. It grows larger every year.

Sun and Sand Facts

The eastern Sahara region is the sunniest place in the world. It has over 4 300 h of sunshine each year.

East central Algeria has the highest sand dunes in the world. The highest dunes measure 430 m.

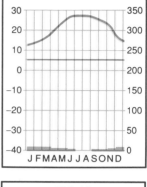

Cairo

Sahara, Niger

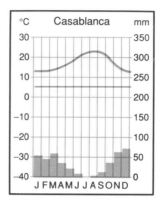

Casablanca

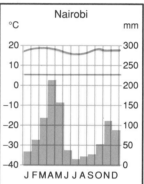

Nairobi

Cameroon

Foothills, Ethiopia

Cape Town

River Facts

The longest river in the world runs through the largest desert area in the world. This river is called the Nile River.

Hex River Valley, South Africa

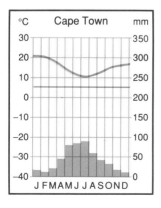

Europe
POLITICAL DIVISIONS

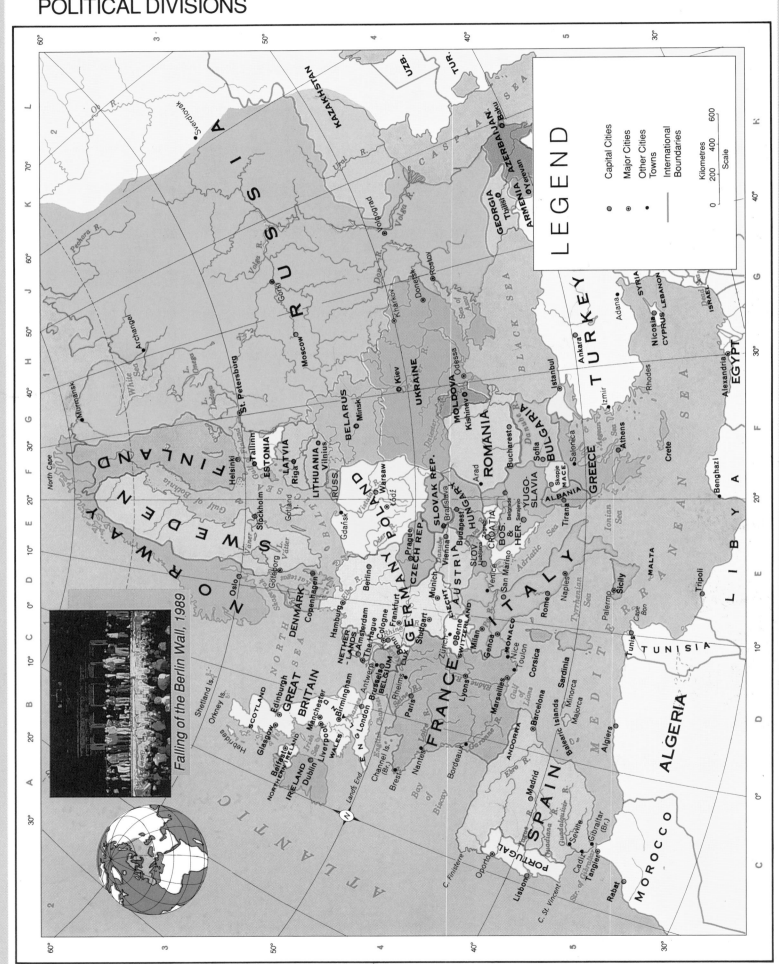

Falling of the Berlin Wall, 1989

LEGEND

- Capital Cities
- Major Cities
- Other Cities
- Towns
- International Boundaries

Kilometres
0 200 400 600
Scale

RUSSIA

KAZAKHSTAN

UZB.

AZERBAIJAN

Baku

Yerevan

ARMENIA

GEORGIA

Tbilisi

TUR.

CASPIAN SEA

Sverdlovsk

Ob R.

Pechora R.

Ural R.

Volga R.

Don R.

Volgograd

Rostov

Donetsk

Kharkov

Sea of Azov

SYRIA

LEBANON

Adana

Nicosia

CYPRUS

ISRAEL

Dead Sea

EGYPT

Alexandria

Archangel

L. Onega

White Sea

Murmansk

North Cape

L. Ladoga

St. Petersburg

Gorki

Moscow

Kiev

UKRAINE

MOLDOVA

Kishinev

Odessa

ROMANIA

Bucharest

Danube R.

Dnieper R.

BLACK SEA

Istanbul

TURKEY

Ankara

Izmir

Rhodes

AEGEAN SEA

Athens

Salonica

Crete

Benghazi

LIBYA

Tripoli

BULGARIA

Sofia

MACE.

Skopje

ALBANIA

Tirana

GREECE

Ionian Sea

MALTA

FINLAND

Helsinki

Gulf of Bothnia

Tallinn

ESTONIA

LATVIA

Riga

LITHUANIA

Vilnius

BELARUS

Minsk

RUSS.

POLAND

Warsaw

Łódź

Gdańsk

Vistula R.

SWEDEN

NORWAY

Oslo

Stockholm

Göteborg

Vänern

Vättern

Gotland I.

BALTIC SEA

Karlstad

DENMARK

Copenhagen

NORTH SEA

Skagerrak

GERMANY

Berlin

Hamburg

Elbe R.

Rhine R.

Frankfurt

Cologne

Stuttgart

Munich

CZECH REP.

Prague

SLOVAK REP.

Bratislava

AUSTRIA

Vienna

HUNGARY

Budapest

Arad

LIECHT.

SLOVENIA

Ljubljana

CROATIA

Zagreb

BOS. &

HER.

Sarajevo

YUGO-

SLAVIA

Belgrade

Adriatic Sea

SWITZERLAND

Berne

Zurich

Venice

San Marino

ITALY

Rome

Naples

Tyrrhenian Sea

Palermo

Sicily

Sardinia

Corsica

MONACO

Nice

Genoa

Milan

Turin

FRANCE

Paris

Rheims

Loire R.

Rhône R.

Nantes

Lyons

Marseilles

Toulon

Bordeaux

Garonne R.

Gulf of Lions

Brest

Bay of Biscay

NETHER-LANDS

Amsterdam

The Hague

LUXEMBOURG

BELGIUM

Brussels

Antwerp

GREAT BRITAIN

ENGLAND

London

Birmingham

Manchester

Liverpool

WALES

SCOTLAND

Edinburgh

Glasgow

IRELAND

NORTHERN IRELAND

Belfast

Dublin

Shetland Is.

Orkney Is.

Hebrides

Channel Is. (Br.)

English Channel

Lands End

Thames R.

ATLANTIC OCEAN

C. Finisterre

SPAIN

Madrid

Barcelona

Balearic Islands

Majorca

Minorca

Ebro R.

Gibraltar (Br.)

Seville

Cadiz

Guadalquivir R.

Guadiana R.

Str. of Gibraltar

Tangier

Rabat

MOROCCO

ALGERIA

Algiers

TUNISIA

Tunis

Str. of Sicily

Cape Bon

MEDITERRANEAN SEA

PORTUGAL

Oporto

Lisbon

C. St. Vincent

ANDORRA

C. Finisterre

Europe
LANDFORMS—Relief

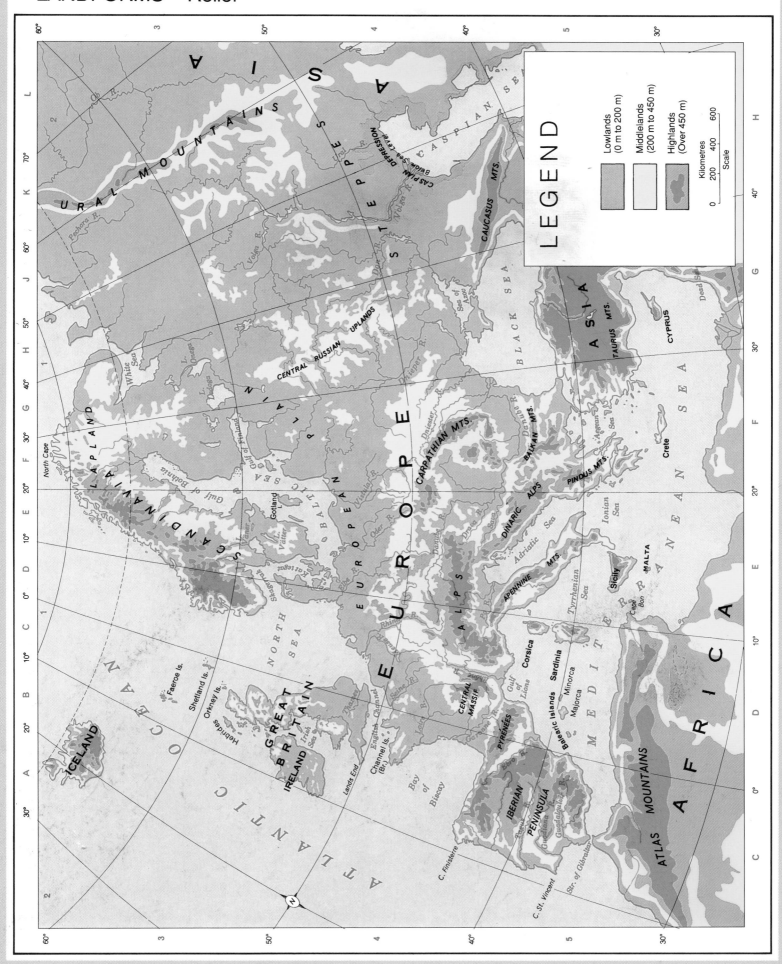

LEGEND

Lowlands (0 m to 200 m)

Middlelands (200 m to 450 m)

Highlands (Over 450 m)

Kilometres
0   200   400   600
Scale

Asia
POLITICAL DIVISIONS

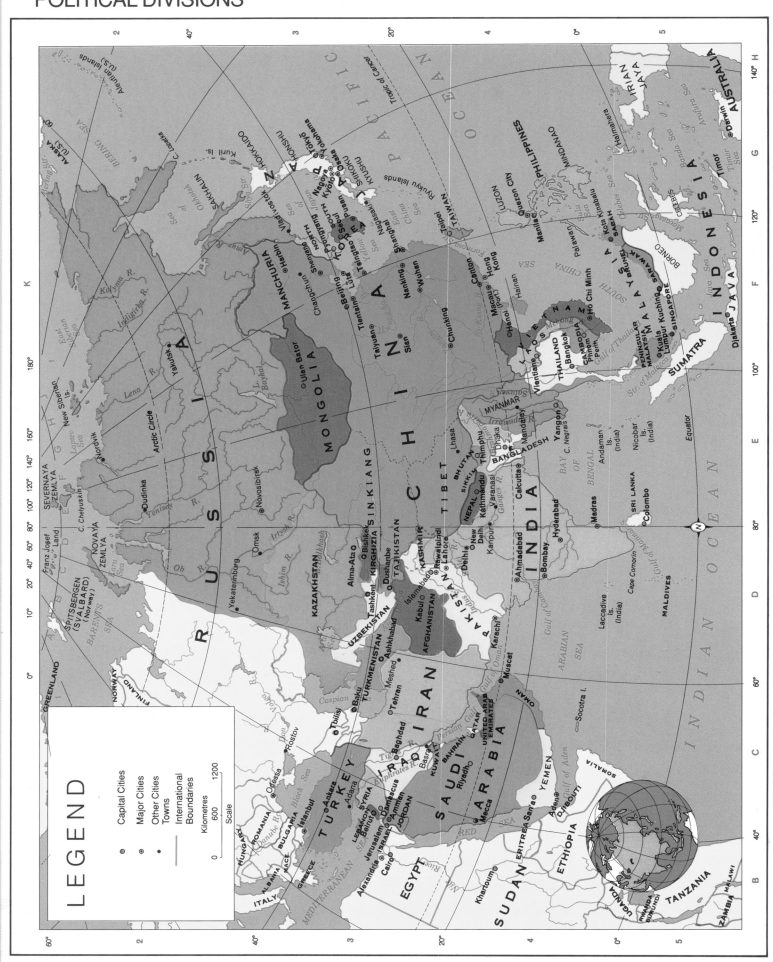

LEGEND

⦿ Capital Cities
◉ Major Cities
• Other Cities
· Towns
— International Boundaries

Scale
Kilometres
0   600   1200

Asia
LANDFORMS—Relief

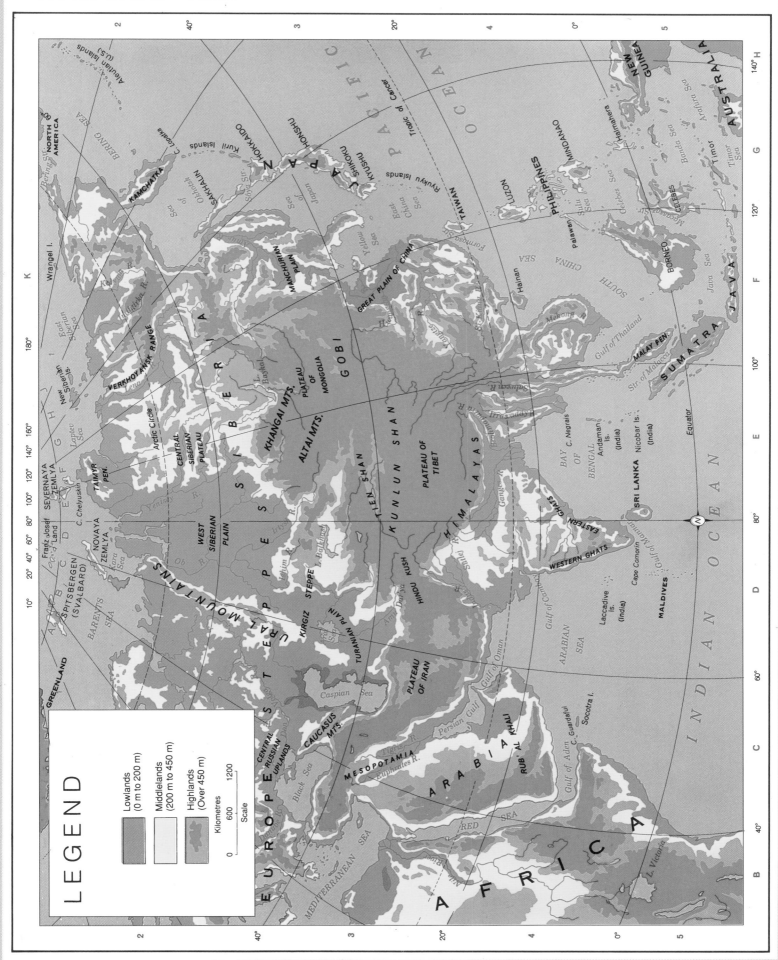

LEGEND

Lowlands (0 m to 200 m)

Middlelands (200 m to 450 m)

Highlands (Over 450 m)

Kilometres

Scale

0   600   1200

Pacific Rim

China

Philippines

ARCTIC OCEAN

RUSSIA

ALASKA (U.S.)

Anchorage

KAZAKHSTAN

MONGOLIA

Vancouver

BERING SEA

Portland

Sea of Okhotsk

Seattle

UZB.

Vladivostok

KIRGHIZIA

Beijing

NORTH KOREA

TUR.

TAJIKISTAN

CHINA

Seoul

JAPAN

San Francisco

AFGHANISTAN

SOUTH KOREA

Tokyo

Los Angeles

PAKISTAN

Osaka

NEPAL

BHUTAN

Shanghai

INDIA

BANGLADESH

Taipei

Hawaii (U.S.)

MYANMAR

TAIWAN

Honolulu

ARABIAN SEA

Bombay

LAOS

HONG KONG

Northern Mariana Islands (U.S.)

BAY OF BENGAL

THAILAND

VIETNAM

Manila

MARSHALL ISLANDS

PACIFIC OCEAN

KAMPUCHEA

CHINA SEA

PHILIPPINES

Guam (U.S.)

SRI LANKA

BRUNEI

Palau (U.S.)

MALAYSIA

EQUATOR

SINGAPORE

BORNEO

Nauru

CELEBES

Kiribati

Jakarta

INDONESIA

PAPUA NEW GUINEA

Solomon Is.

Tokelau (N.Z.)

INDIAN OCEAN

Tuvalu

Wallis and Futuna (France)

W. Samoa

French Polynesia (France)

Vanuatu

Am. Samoa (U.S.)

Fiji

Cook Islands (N.Z.)

Niue (N.Z.)

AUSTRALIA

New Caledonia (Fr.)

Tonga

Pitcairn

Brisbane

Sydney

TASMAN SEA

Melbourne

Tasmania

New Zealand

Kerguelen I. (Fr.)

international date line

Antarctica

LEGEND

○ Capital Cities

● Principal Cities

Kilometres

0 500 1000

Scale

60°E 90°E 120°E 150°E 180° 150°W 120°W 90°W

60°N

30°N

0°

30°S

60°S

Canada

Main Languages of the Rim

Country	Language Spoken
Argentina	Spanish
Chile	Spanish
Peru	Spanish
Ecuador	Spanish
Colombia	Spanish
Panama	Spanish
Costa Rica	Spanish
Nicaragua	Spanish
El Salvador	Spanish
Guatemala	Spanish
Mexico	Spanish
United States	English
Canada	English, French
Russia	Russian
China	Chinese
Japan	Japanese
Korea	Korean
Vietnam	Vietnamese, French
Indonesia	Bahasa, Indonesian
Malaysia	Malay, Chinese
Philippines	Tagalog, English
New Guinea	Papuan
Australia	English
New Zealand	English

Within each country, many native languages and dialects exist.

Mexico

Ecuador

Australasia
POLITICAL DIVISIONS

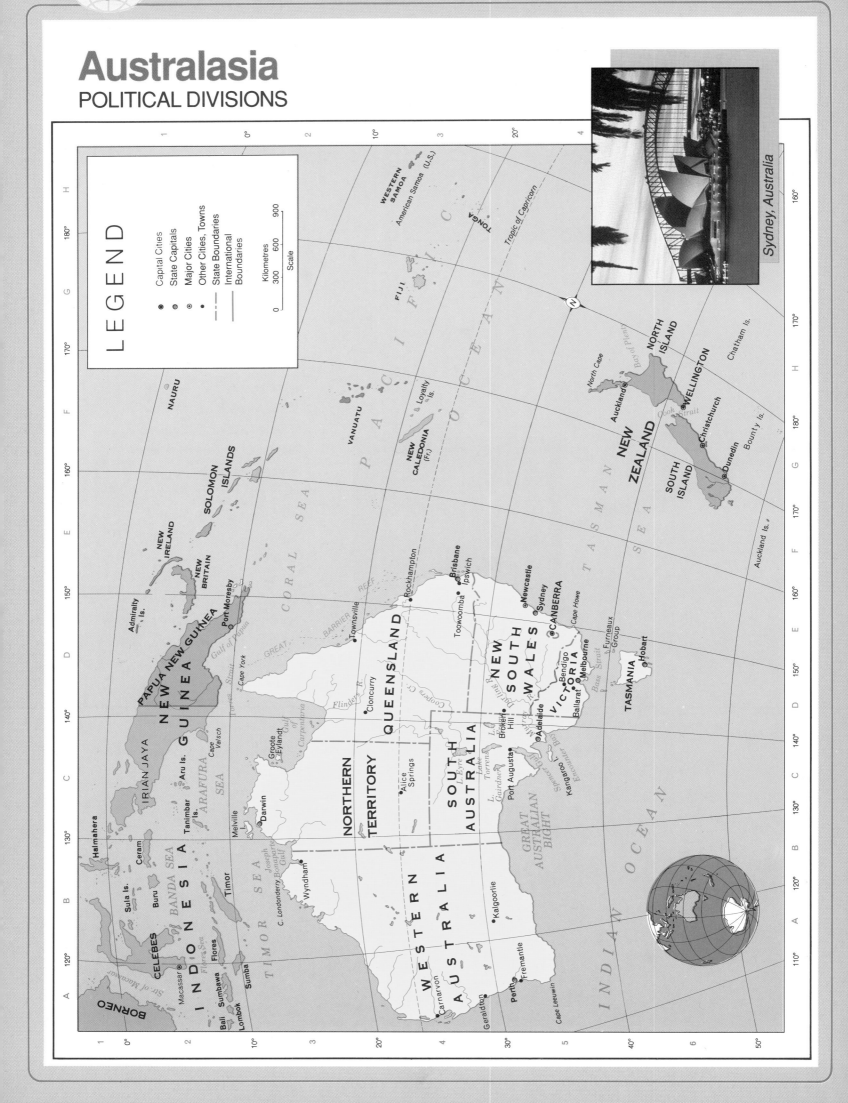

Sydney, Australia

LEGEND

- Capital Cities
- State Capitals
- Major Cities
- Other Cities, Towns
- –·–·– State Boundaries
- —— International Boundaries

Kilometres
0 300 600 900
Scale

PACIFIC OCEAN

WESTERN SAMOA
American Samoa (U.S.)
TONGA
Tropic of Capricorn
FIJI
VANUATU
NEW CALEDONIA (Fr.)
Loyalty Is.

NAURU
SOLOMON ISLANDS
NEW IRELAND
NEW BRITAIN
Admiralty Is.
PAPUA NEW GUINEA
Port Moresby
Gulf of Papua
IRIAN JAYA

HALMAHERA
Sula Is.
Ceram
Buru
BANDA SEA
CELEBES
MACASSAR
Str. of Macassar
INDONESIA
Flores Sea
Bali Sumbawa Flores
Lombok Sumba
BORNEO

Tanimbar Is.
Aru Is.
ARAFURA SEA
Cape Valsch
TIMOR SEA
Timor
Melville I.
Melville L.
Darwin
Wyndham
C. Londonderry
Bonaparte Gulf
Joseph Bonaparte Gulf
Cape York
Torres Strait
Groote Eylandt
Gulf of Carpentaria
Flinders R.

CORAL SEA
GREAT BARRIER REEF
Townsville
Rockhampton
Brisbane
Ipswich
Cloncurry
Cooper Cr.
Toowoomba
Newcastle
Sydney
CANBERRA

NORTHERN TERRITORY
Alice Springs
QUEENSLAND
NEW SOUTH WALES
Broken Hill
Murray R.
Darling R.
VICTORIA
Bendigo
Ballarat
Melbourne

WESTERN AUSTRALIA
SOUTH AUSTRALIA
L. Eyre
Lake Gairdner
L. Torrens
Port Augusta
Adelaide
Kangaroo I.
Encounter Bay
Spencer Gulf
Gulf St. Vincent

GREAT AUSTRALIAN BIGHT
Kalgoorlie
Perth
Fremantle
Carnarvon
Geraldton
Cape Leeuwin

INDIAN OCEAN

TASMAN SEA
Cape Howe
Furneaux Group
Bass Strait
TASMANIA
Hobart

NEW ZEALAND
NORTH ISLAND
Bay of Plenty
North Cape
Auckland
Cook Strait
WELLINGTON
Christchurch
SOUTH ISLAND
Dunedin
Chatham Is.
Bounty Is.
Auckland Is.

N

Australasia
LANDFORMS—Relief

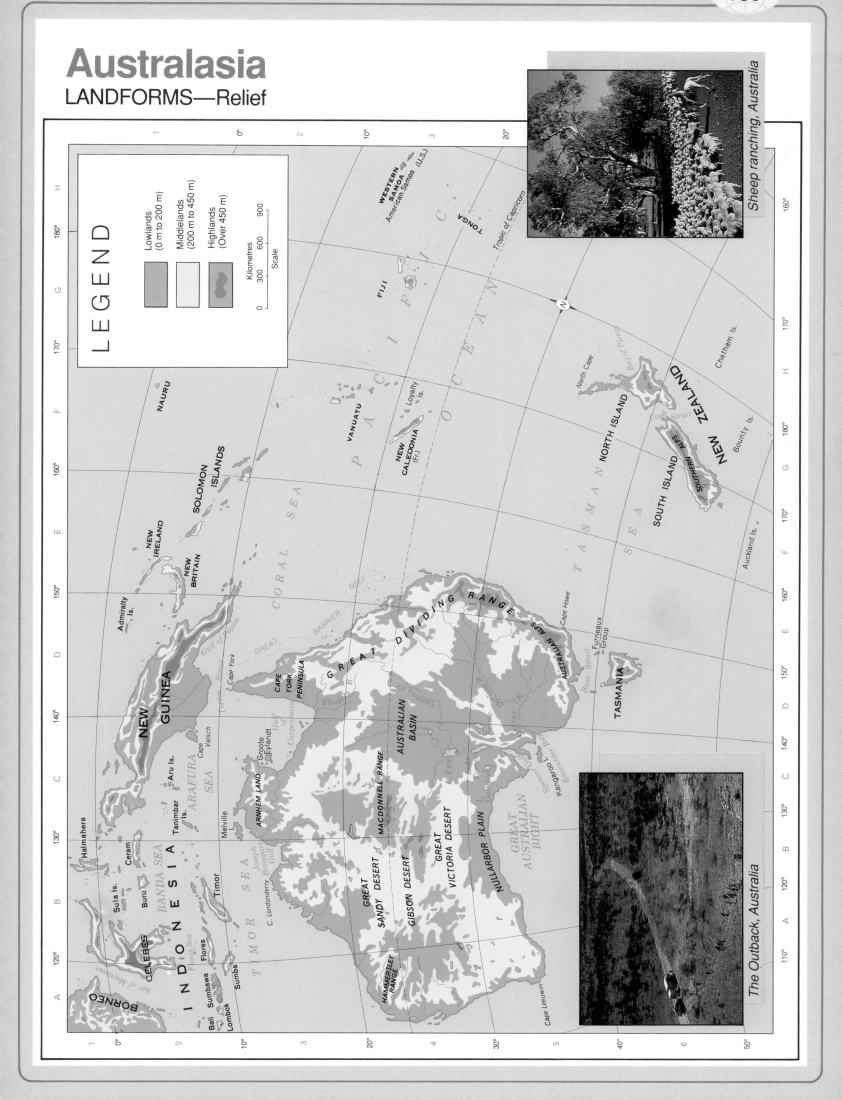

LEGEND

Lowlands (0 m to 200 m)
Middlelands (200 m to 450 m)
Highlands (Over 450 m)

Kilometres
0 300 600 900
Scale

Sheep ranching, Australia

The Outback, Australia

PACIFIC OCEAN

WESTERN SAMOA
American Samoa (U.S.)
TONGA
Tropic of Capricorn
FIJI
VANUATU
NEW CALEDONIA (Fr.)
Loyalty Is.

NAURU
NEW IRELAND
NEW BRITAIN
SOLOMON ISLANDS
Admiralty Is.

NEW GUINEA
Gulf of Papua
Cape York
Torres Strait
Flinders R.

CORAL SEA
GREAT BARRIER REEF

TASMAN SEA

North Cape
Bay of Plenty
NORTH ISLAND
Cook Strait
SOUTH ISLAND
SOUTHERN ALPS
NEW ZEALAND
Chatham Is.
Bounty Is.
Auckland Is.

Halmahera
Sula Is.
Buru
Ceram
BANDA SEA
CELEBES
BORNEO
INDONESIA
Flores Sea
Bali Sumbawa
Lombok
Sumba
Flores
Timor
Str. of Macassar
TIMOR SEA
ARAFURA SEA
Tanimbar Is.
Aru Is.
Cape Valsch
Melville I.
Groote Eylandt
ARNHEM LAND
Gulf of Carpentaria
Joseph Bonaparte Gulf
C. Londonderry

CAPE YORK PENINSULA
GREAT DIVIDING RANGE
AUSTRALIAN ALPS
Cape Howe
Furneaux Group
Bass Strait
TASMANIA

AUSTRALIAN BASIN
MACDONNELL RANGE
GREAT SANDY DESERT
GIBSON DESERT
GREAT VICTORIA DESERT
HAMERSLEY RANGE
NULLARBOR PLAIN
GREAT AUSTRALIAN BIGHT
Spencer Gulf
Kangaroo I.
Encounter Bay
Cape Leeuwin

Antarctica

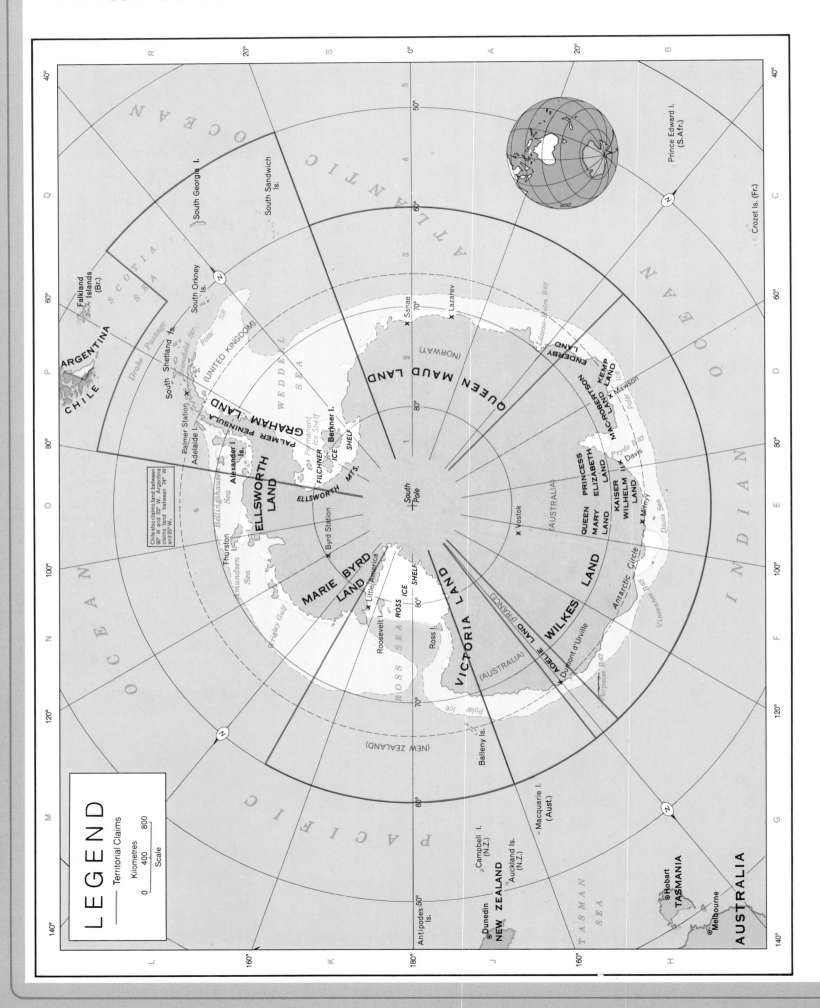

Ozone Facts

The damaging ultra-violet rays which come from the sun are absorbed by a layer of ozone high above Earth. In recent years, scientists have discovered that this layer over the poles has grown thinner than it once was. Between 1979 and 1986, the average global ozone levels dropped by 5 percent.

Penguins, Antarctica

Antarctic Research Station

The Arctic

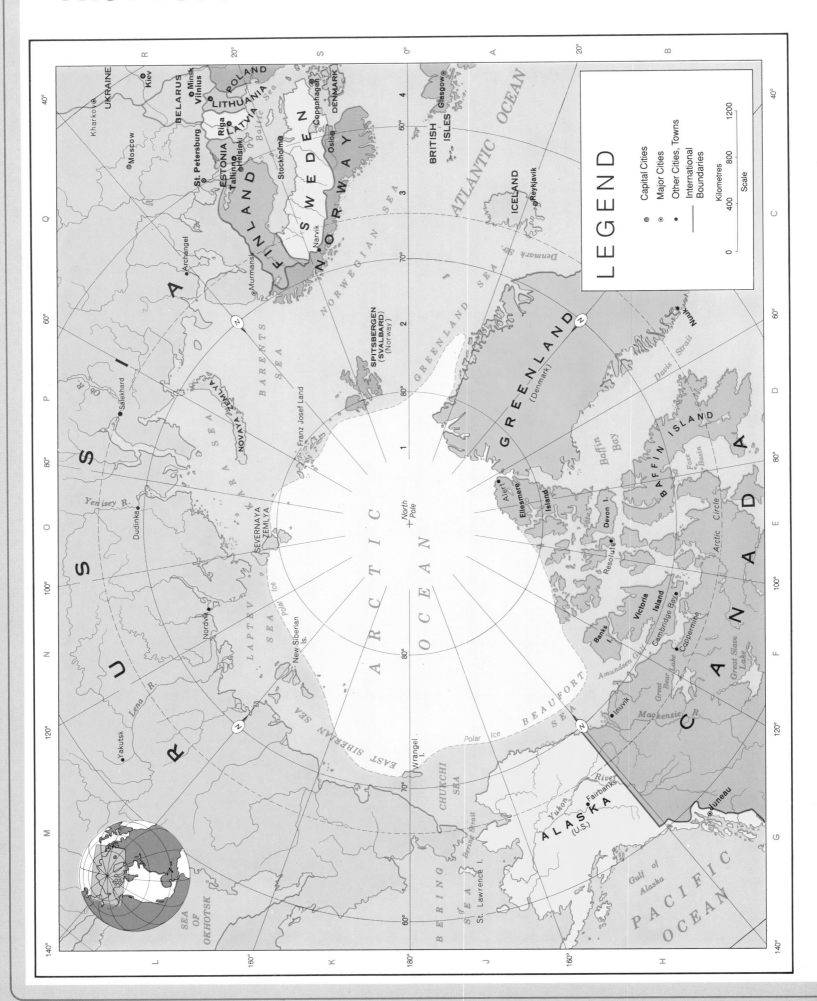

LEGEND

- ● Capital Cities
- ◉ Major Cities
- • Other Cities, Towns
- —— International Boundaries

Kilometres

0   400   800   1200

Scale

Seals, The Arctic

The North West Territories

Walrus, The Arctic

World Exploration

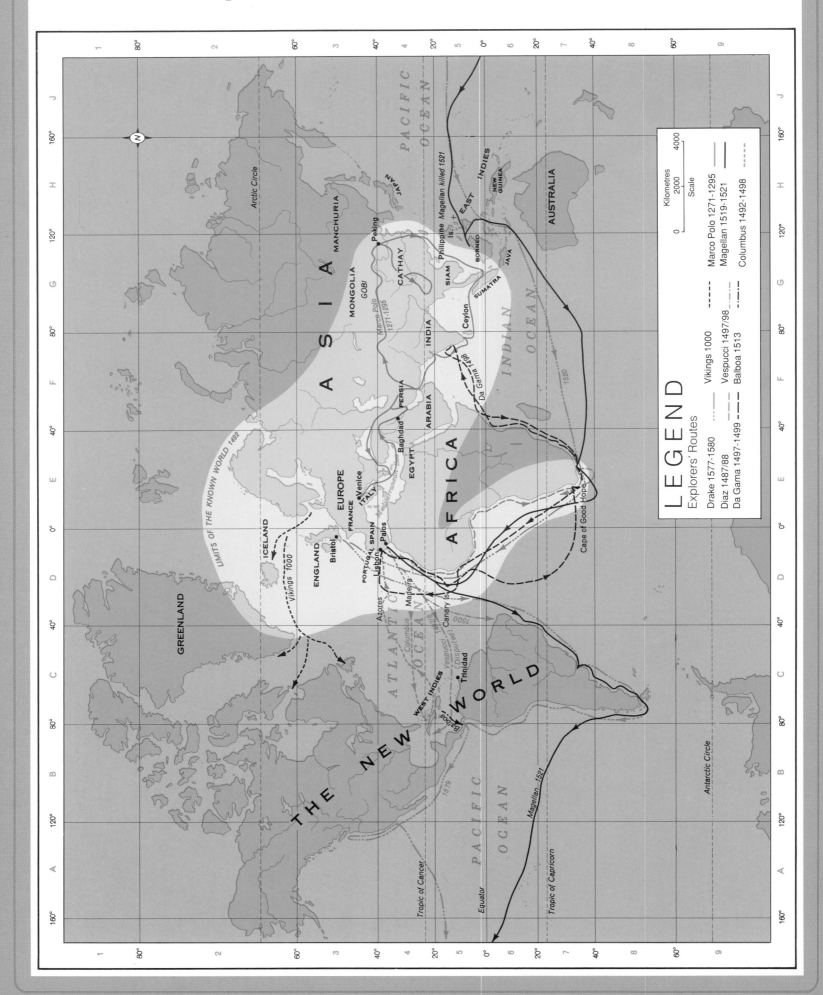

Explorers

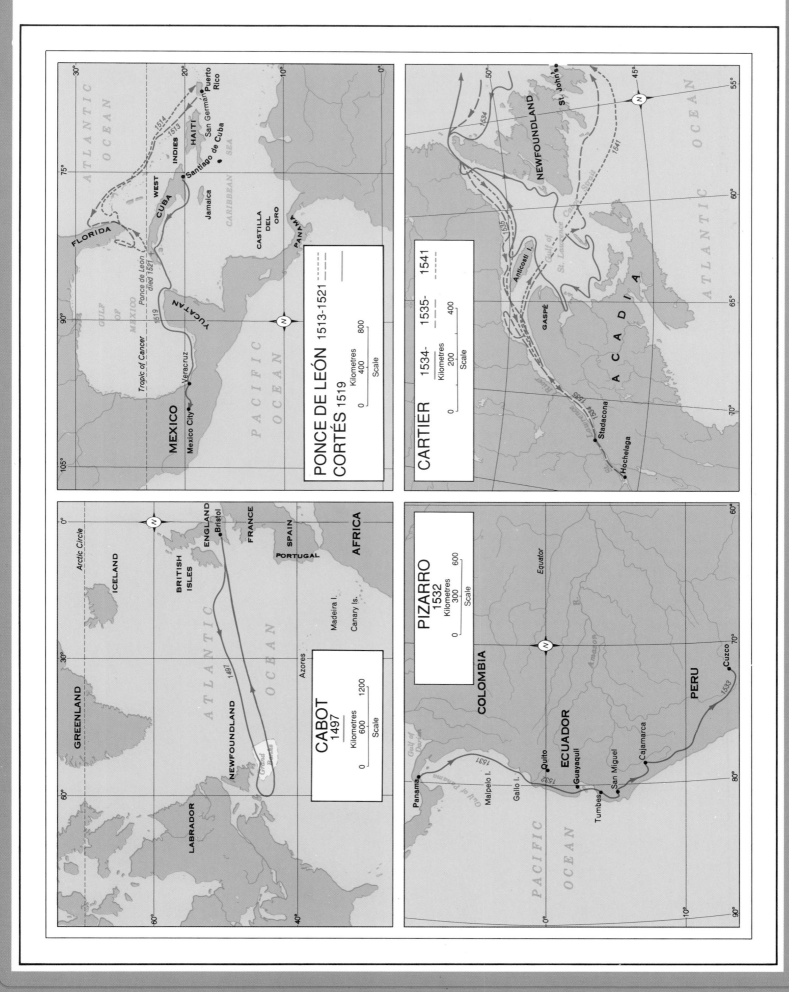

PONCE DE LEÓN 1513-1521 ------
CORTÉS 1519 ——

Scale
Kilometres
0   400   800

ATLANTIC OCEAN

Puerto Rico
San Germán
HAITI
WEST INDIES
Santiago
CUBA
Jamaica
CARIBBEAN SEA
CASTILLA DEL ORO
PANAMA
FLORIDA
GULF OF MEXICO
Ponce de León died 1521
Tropic of Cancer
YUCATAN
MEXICO
Mexico City
Veracruz
PACIFIC OCEAN

CARTIER
1534- ——
1535- ———
1541 ------

Scale
Kilometres
0   200   400

NEWFOUNDLAND
St. John's
ATLANTIC OCEAN
Gulf of St. Lawrence
Anticosti I.
ACADIA
GASPÉ
St. Lawrence River
Stadacona
Hochelaga

CABOT
1497

Scale
Kilometres
0   600   1200

Arctic Circle
GREENLAND
ICELAND
BRITISH ISLES
ENGLAND
Bristol
FRANCE
SPAIN
PORTUGAL
AFRICA
Madeira I.
Canary Is.
Azores
ATLANTIC OCEAN
NEWFOUNDLAND
Grand Banks
LABRADOR

PIZARRO
1532

Scale
Kilometres
0   300   600

COLOMBIA
Equator
Amazon R.
ECUADOR
Quito
Guayaquil
PERU
Cuzco
Cajamarca
San Miguel
Tumbes
Gallo I.
Malpelo I.
Gulf of Panama
Panama
Gulf of Darien
PACIFIC OCEAN

Explorers

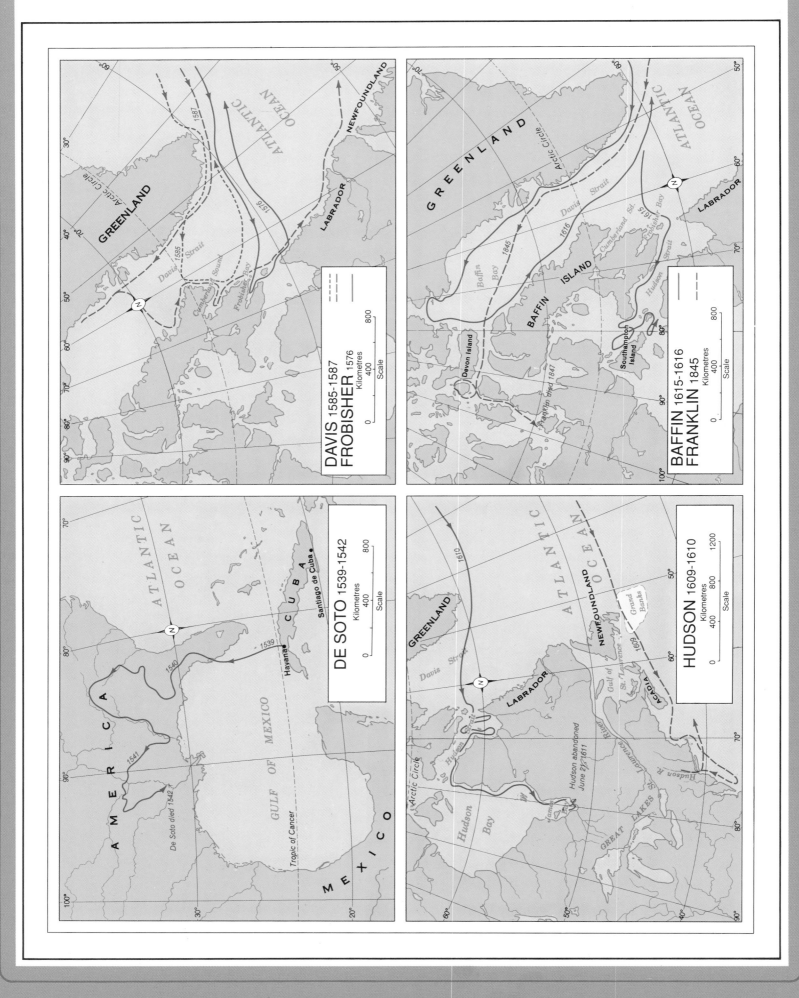

DAVIS 1585-1587
FROBISHER 1576
Kilometres
Scale
0 400 800

BAFFIN 1615-1616
FRANKLIN 1845
Kilometres
Scale
0 400 800

DE SOTO 1539-1542
Kilometres
Scale
0 400 800

HUDSON 1609-1610
Kilometres
Scale
0 400 800 1200

Explorers

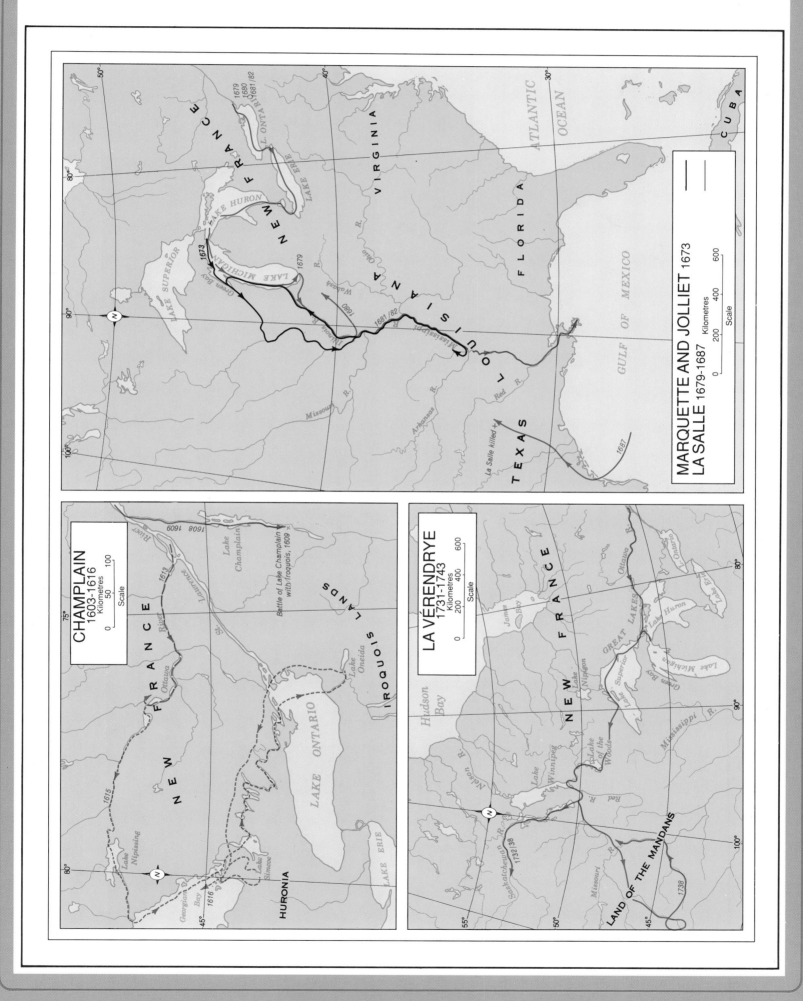

Explorers

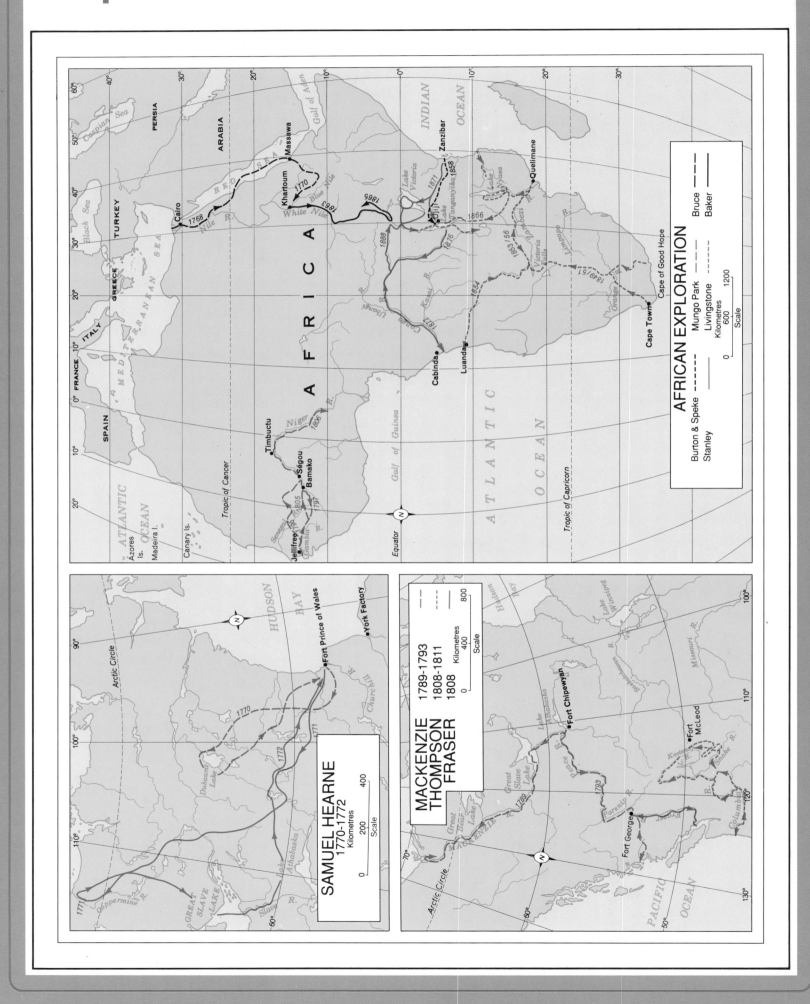

AFRICAN EXPLORATION

Burton & Speke
Stanley
Mungo Park
Livingstone
Bruce
Baker

Scale
Kilometres
0   600   1200

SAMUEL HEARNE
1770-1772

Scale
Kilometres
0   200   400

MACKENZIE   1789-1793
THOMPSON   1808-1811
FRASER   1808

Scale
Kilometres
0   400   800

Polar Exploration

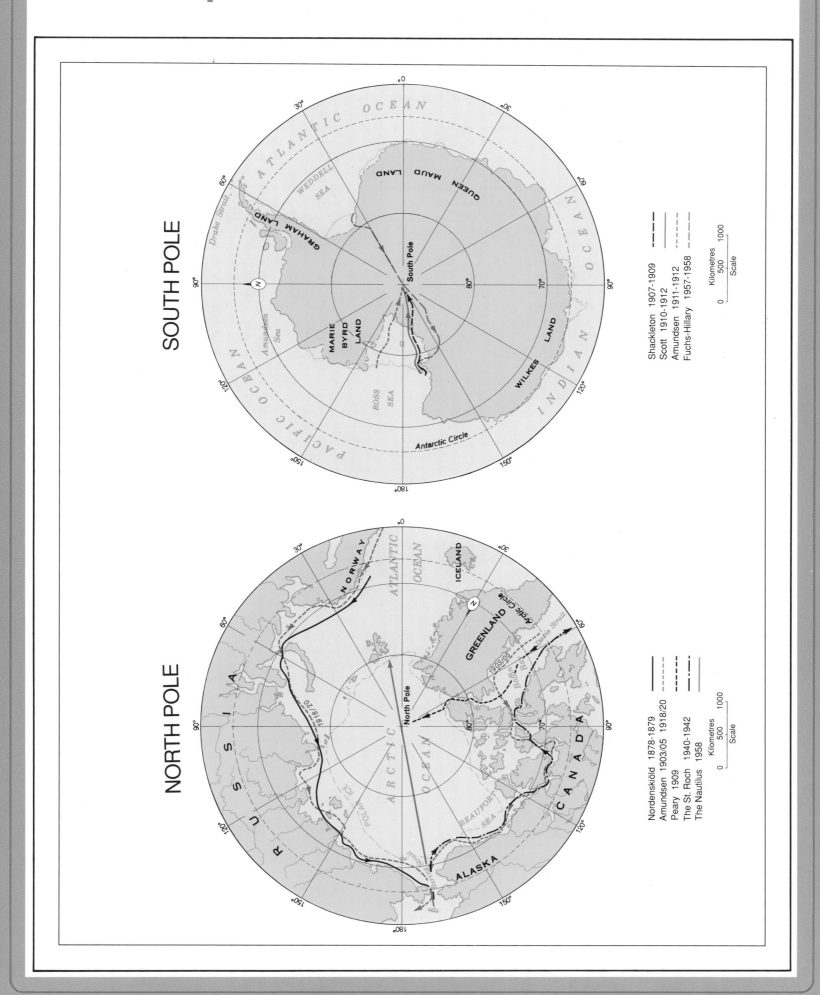

SOUTH POLE

ATLANTIC OCEAN

WEDDELL SEA

QUEEN MAUD LAND

GRAHAM LAND

Drake Strait

PACIFIC OCEAN

Amundsen Sea

MARIE BYRD LAND

South Pole

INDIAN OCEAN

WILKES LAND

ROSS SEA

Antarctic Circle

Shackleton 1907-1909
Scott 1910-1912
Amundsen 1911-1912
Fuchs-Hillary 1957-1958

Kilometres
0   500   1000
Scale

NORTH POLE

NORWAY

ATLANTIC OCEAN

ICELAND

GREENLAND

Arctic Circle

1903/04

Baffin Bay

Davis Strait

RUSSIA

1918/20

North Pole

POLAR ICE

ARCTIC OCEAN

BEAUFORT SEA

CANADA

ALASKA

Nordenskiöld 1878-1879
Amundsen 1903/05 1918/20
Peary 1909
The St. Roch 1940-1942
The Nautilus 1958

Kilometres
0   500   1000
Scale

North America
NATIVE PEOPLES—1500

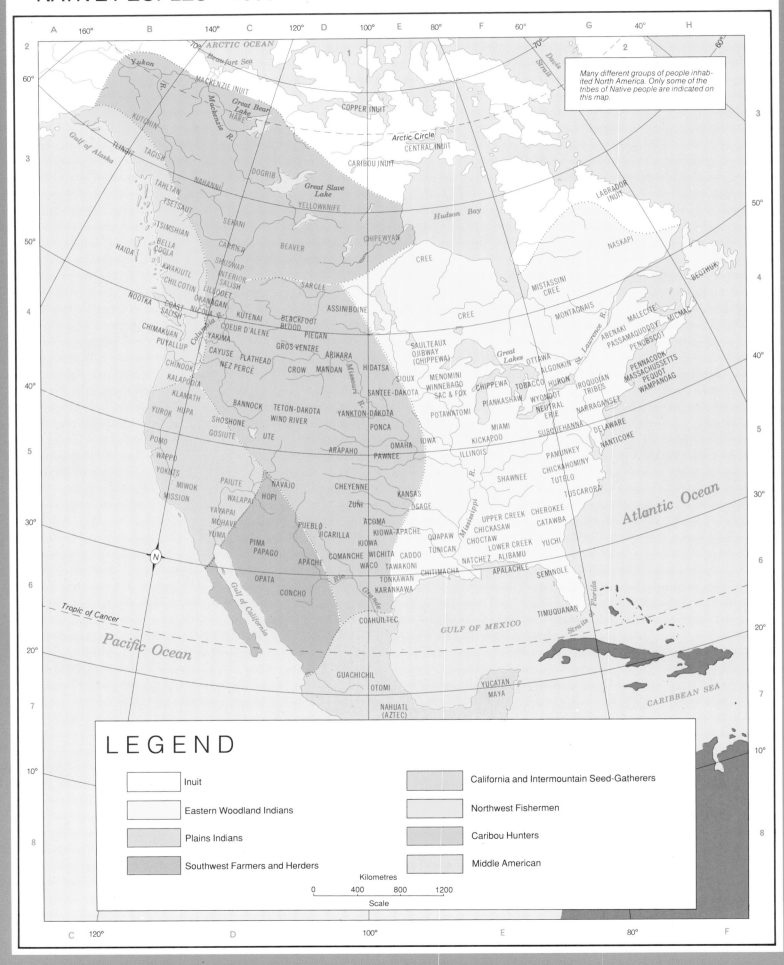

Canada
LIFESTYLES OF NATIVE PEOPLES—1500

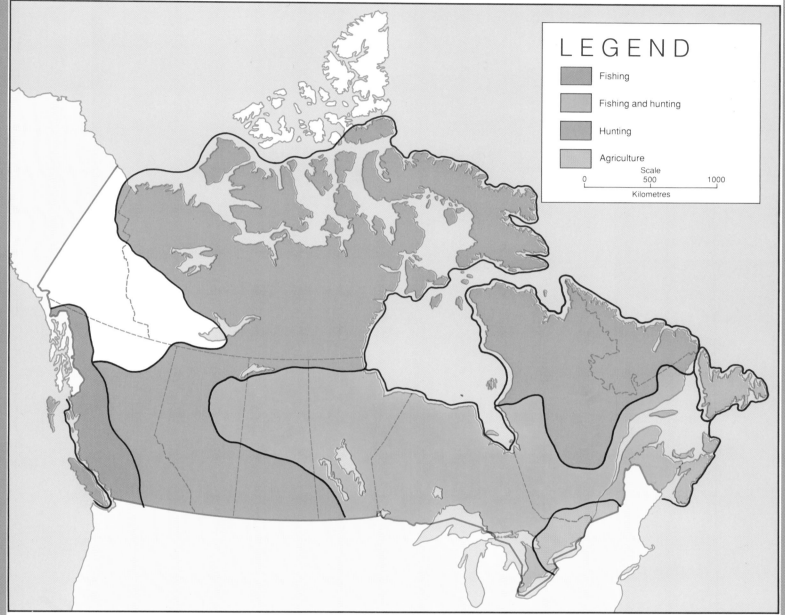

LEGEND

Fishing

Fishing and hunting

Hunting

Agriculture

Scale

0   500   1000

Kilometres

West Coast Indians Returning from the Hunt,
painting by Thomas Mower Martin

A Buffalo Pound, engraving by Edw. Finden

Canada
NATIVE PEOPLES—TODAY

Dakota, Alberta

Cowichan, British Columbia

Where Native Peoples Live

Newfoundland	1.8
Prince Edward Island	0.1
Nova Scotia	1.6
New Brunswick	1.3
Quebec	8.9
Ontario	17.7
Manitoba	16.1
Saskatchewan	13.9
Alberta	15.4
British Columbia	17.5
Yukon	0.8
Northwest Territories and Nunavut	4.9

= 100%

Cree, Saskatchewan

LEGEND
Major Linguistic Groups

- Algonkian
- Athapascan
- Haida
- Iroquoian
- Kootenayan
- Salishan
- Siouan
- Tlingit
- Tsimshian
- Waskashan
- Inuktituk

Canadian Native Peoples Population 1996				
	Total Aboriginal Population	Native Indian	Metis	Inuit
Canada	799 010	554 290	210 190	41 080
Newfoundland	14 205	5 430	4 685	4 265
Prince Edward Island	950	825	120	15
Nova Scotia	12 380	11 340	860	210
New Brunswick	10 250	9 180	975	120
Quebec	71 415	47 600	16 075	8 300
Ontario	141 525	118 830	22 790	1 300
Manitoba	128 685	82 990	46 195	360
Saskatchewan	111 245	75 205	36 535	190
Alberta	122 840	72 645	50 745	795
British Columbia	139 655	113 315	26 750	815
Yukon	6 175	5 530	565	110
Northwest Territories and Nunavut	39 690	11 400	3 895	24 600

There is some discrepancy in the above numbers as some people responded to the questionnaire by stating they belonged to more than one aboriginal group.

Micmac, Cape Breton Island, Nova Scotia

Inuk, North West Territories

North America
AREAS OF COLONIAL INFLUENCE—1664

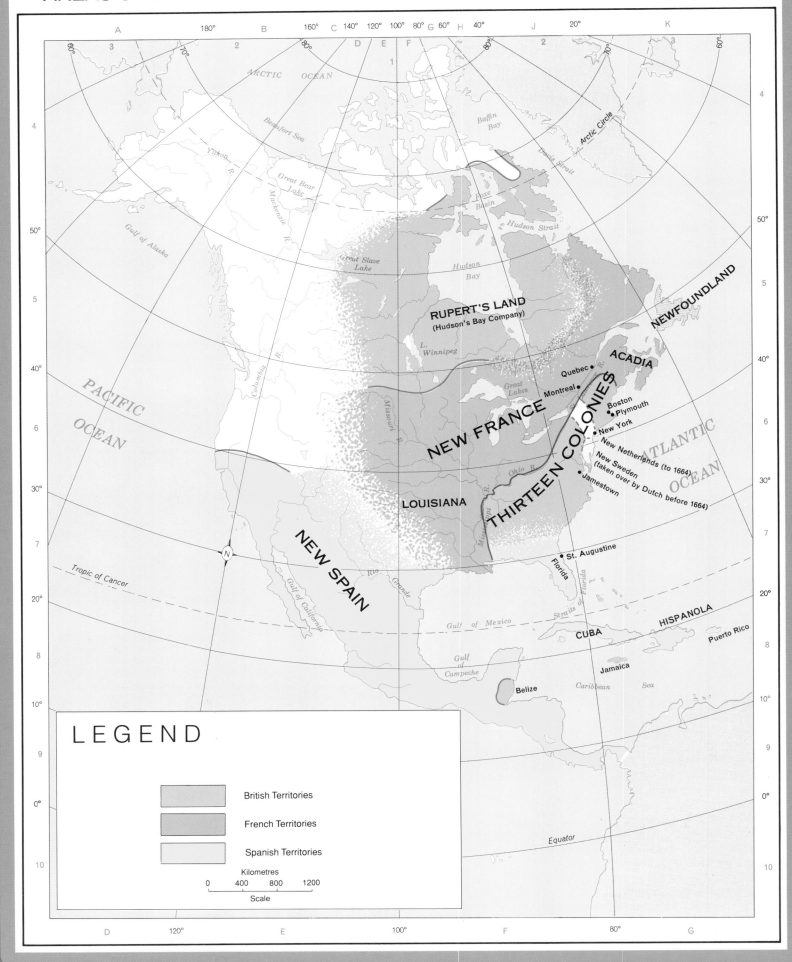

ARCTIC OCEAN

Beaufort Sea

Baffin Bay

Arctic Circle

Davis Strait

Yukon R.

Great Bear Lake

Mackenzie R.

Foxe Basin

Hudson Strait

Gulf of Alaska

Great Slave Lake

Hudson Bay

NEWFOUNDLAND

RUPERT'S LAND
(Hudson's Bay Company)

L. Winnipeg

ACADIA

PACIFIC OCEAN

Columbia R.

Great Lakes

Quebec

Montreal

NEW FRANCE

Missouri R.

Boston
Plymouth

New York

New Netherlands (to 1664)

New Sweden
(taken over by Dutch before 1664)

ATLANTIC OCEAN

THIRTEEN COLONIES

Ohio R.

LOUISIANA

Mississippi R.

Jamestown

N

St. Augustine

Florida

NEW SPAIN

Tropic of Cancer

Rio Grande

Gulf of California

Straits of Florida

HISPANOLA

Gulf of Mexico

CUBA

Puerto Rico

Gulf of Campeche

Jamaica

Belize

Caribbean Sea

Equator

LEGEND

British Territories

French Territories

Spanish Territories

Kilometres

0   400   800   1200

Scale

Canada
POLITICAL DEVELOPMENT

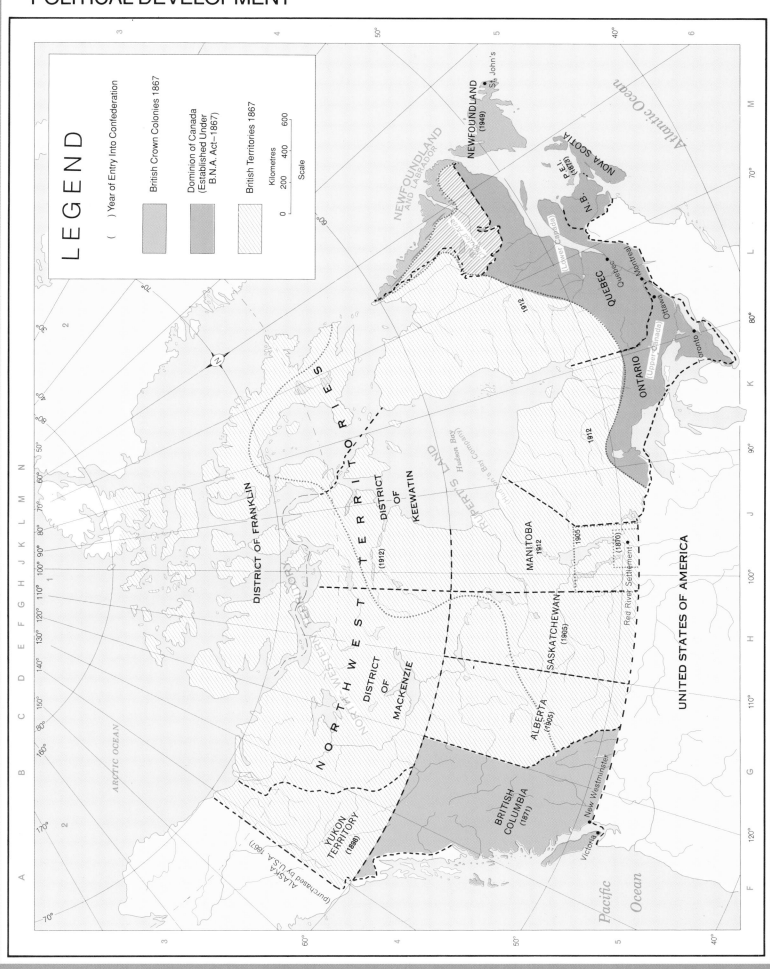

LEGEND

( ) Year of Entry Into Confederation

British Crown Colonies 1867

Dominion of Canada (Established Under B.N.A. Act—1867)

British Territories 1867

Scale

Kilometres

0   200   400   600

Atlantic Ocean

NEWFOUNDLAND AND LABRADOR

NEWFOUNDLAND (1949)

St. John's

NOVA SCOTIA

P.E.I. (1873)

N.B.

RUPERT'S LAND

(Lower Canada)

QUEBEC

Quebec

Montreal

Ottawa

(Upper Canada)

ONTARIO

Toronto

DISTRICT OF FRANKLIN

NORTHWESTERN TERRITORY

DISTRICT OF KEEWATIN

DISTRICT OF MACKENZIE

(1912)

1912

Hudson Bay

Hudson's Bay Company

MANITOBA 1912

1905

(1870)

Red River Settlement

SASKATCHEWAN (1905)

ALBERTA (1905)

YUKON TERRITORY (1898)

BRITISH COLUMBIA (1871)

New Westminster

Victoria

ARCTIC OCEAN

ALASKA (purchased by U.S.A. 1867)

UNITED STATES OF AMERICA

Pacific Ocean

Gazetteer

On the following pages are two alphabetical lists of all the important names that appear on the maps in this atlas. The first list is of Canadian names. The other is of the rest of the world.

Names are generally followed by the name of the country, continent, or ocean in which they are situated. The Canadian names, however, only include the name of the province in which the place is found. Those names that appear more than once are indexed only once.

After each name there is a figure that shows the page number of the map on which you will find the place. Following this is a letter and another figure. These refer to the letters along the top and bottom of each map and to the figures along each side. Together they will help you find the position of any place on the map.

Physical features are also listed in the gazetteer. Each feature is abbreviated, set in italics, and followed by the term indicating its nature. Also, names of countries may appear in an abbreviated form on a map. Some examples appear below and others are shown with underlining on the pages that follow.

Names appearing more than once are listed in this order: first, place names; second, political divisions; and third, physical features.

ABBREVIATIONS

Afghan.	Afghanistan
Ala.	Alabama
Alsk.	Alaska
Alta.	Alberta
Antarc.	Antarctica
arch.	archipelago
Arc. Oc.	Arctic Ocean
Ariz.	Arizona
At. Oc.	Atlantic Ocean
Aust.	Australia

b.	bay
bas.	basin
B.C.	British Columbia

c.	cape
Calif.	California
C.A.R.	Central African Republic
C. Am.	Central America
Can.	Canada
Carib. S.	Caribbean Sea
ch.	channel
Congo Rep.	Congo Republic
Conn.	Connecticut
cur.	current
Cz.	Czech Republic

Dem.	Democratic
Den.	Denmark
des.	desert
dist.	district
Dom. Rep.	Dominican Republic

Eur.	Europe

f.	feature
Fla.	Florida
Fr.	France, French

g.	gulf
G. of Mex.	Gulf of Mexico
Guat.	Guatemala

Hon.	Honduras

i., Is., *is.*	island(s)
Ill.	Illinois
in.	inlet
Ind. Oc.	Indian Ocean
isth.	isthmus

l., L., *ls.*	lake(s)
Louis.	Louisiana

Man.	Manitoba
Mass.	Massachusetts
Md.	Maryland
Med. S.	Mediterranean Sea
Mex.	Mexico
Mich.	Michigan
Minn.	Minnesota
Miss.	Mississippi
mt., Mt., *mts.*	mountain(s)

N.	North, Northern; New
N. Am.	North America
N.B.	New Brunswick
N.C.	North Carolina
N.D.	North Dakota
Neb.	Nebraska
Neth.	Netherlands
Nfld.	Newfoundland
N.H.	New Hampshire
Nic.	Nicaragua
N.J.	New Jersey
N. Mex.	New Mexico
N.S.	Nova Scotia
Nun.	Nunavut
N.W.T.	Northwest Territories
N.Y.	New York
N.Z.	New Zealand

Okla.	Oklahoma
Ont.	Ontario

Pa.	Pennsylvania
Pac. Oc.	Pacific Ocean
Pak.	Pakistan
P.E.I.	Prince Edward Island
pen.	peninsula
Port.	Portuguese
prov.	province
pt.	point

Que.	Quebec

r.	river
reg.	region
rep., Rep.	republic
res.	reservoir
res. stat.	research station

s., S.	sea, Sea; South
S. Am.	South America
Sask.	Saskatchewan
S.C.	South Carolina
sd.	sound
S.D.	South Dakota
S.I.	Slovak Republic
Sp.	Spain, Spanish
St., Ste.	Saint(e)
str.	strait
S.W.	South West
Switz.	Switzerland

Tas.	Tasmania
Tenn.	Tennessee
terr., Terr.	territory
Tex.	Texas

U.S.A.	United States of America

Venez.	Venezuela

W.	West
Wash.	Washington
W. Virg.	West Virginia

Zimb.	Zimbabwe